A **FRESH EXPRESSIONS** BOOK

LEONARD SWEET & MICHAEL ADAM BECK

CONTEXTUAL INTELLIGENCE

UNLOCKING THE ANCIENT SECRET TO MISSION ON THE FRONT LINES

Contextual Intelligence: Unlocking the Ancient Secret to Mission on the Front Lines
By Leonard Sweet and Michael Beck
Copyright © 2020 Leonard Sweet, Michael Beck

ISBN-13: 978-1-951492-32-8
ISBN- eBook: 978-1-951492-33-5

Library of Congress Case# 1-9081238351

Published by HigherLife Development Services, Inc.
PO Box 623307
Oviedo, Florida 32762
(407) 563-4806
www.ahigherlife.com

Unless otherwise noted, all Scripture quotations are taken from the New Revised Standard Version of the Bible. Copyright © 1989 by the Division of Christian Education of the National Council of the Churches of Christ in the USA. Used by permission.

Scripture quotations marked NIV are taken from the Holy Bible, New International Version®, NIV®. Copyright © 1973, 1978, 1984, 2011 by Biblica, Inc.® Used by permission of Zondervan. All rights reserved worldwide. www.zondervan.com. The "NIV" and "New International Version" are trademarks registered in the United States Patent and Trademark Office by Biblica, Inc.®

Scripture quotations marked MSG are from The Message: The Bible in Contemporary English, copyright © 1993, 1994, 1995, 1996, 2000, 2001, 2002. Used by permission of NavPress Publishing Group.

Printed in the United States of America
10 9 8 7 6 5 4 3 2 1

CONTENTS ON THE TABLE

PART I

READING THE SIGNS

(EVALUATION)

Of Issachar, *those who had understanding of the times, to know what Israel ought to do,* and all their kindred under their command.

—1 CHRONICLES 12:32, ITALICS OURS

CHAPTER 1

THREE VIGNETTES

These opening vignettes are representative of who this book is for.

1. Cynthia is an ordained clergyperson in a mainline denomination. As an itinerant preacher, she has been successful at a series of revitalization appointments. Each church she has served has grown, and the episcopacy has noticed her gifts to lead congregations from decline into revitalization. She is deployed to a new appointment, full of hope that this will be another church that flourishes under her guidance.

   Only it doesn't. She is a gifted preacher who spends many hours each week preparing sermons. She spends a good deal of time in the office, making herself accessible to the congregation. She visits the sick in the hospital and the matriarchs of the congregation in their homes. She does all the things she did in previous appointments where churches began to thrive. None of it works. The congregation continues to decline and is now in a conversation about closure.

2. A once thriving global denomination has been in decline for several decades. Most of its churches have plateaued or are on the brink of

closure. Many have had no baptisms and no reception of new disciples in years. Even those that are growing seem to be taking advantage of migrations of churched Christians to new areas. On top of the decline, several divisive issues now threaten to tear the denomination apart.

A small working party consisting of bishops, clergy, and laypersons is chosen to create a series of plans for how the denomination can move forward without schism. Their work is focused primarily on a handful of specific issues and how to organize appropriate responses. At the global gathering, the plans are presented, followed by utter chaos breaking loose. The denomination is now on the brink of serious schism or even death.

3. John is a nondenominational pastor in an autonomous congregational church system. He was young when he started in ministry and has since served two large, thriving churches in his ten-year career. At each church, he has focused on building strong youth programs and attracting young families. He receives a call from a large legacy church in a beautiful part of the southern United States. This church has been through a significant visioning process, and they have concluded that they need a young pastor who can attract families and build a youth program. John interviews with the elders, and they commit to hire him on the spot with a significant pay increase.

John and his family move to the area, full of excitement to make new friends and help this church grow. John employs all his old tools, hanging out in targeted locations throughout the community to connect with new people, visiting significant leaders in the church, hiring the best youth pastor he could find, and planning big community gatherings to get people to the church grounds. All his tactics fail epically; he can't seem to locate or make meaningful relationships with people under fifty. Not only does he not attract young families, he offends some of the older members. These folks are large financial contributors, but they become aggravated by John's pyrotechnic preaching and endless stream of new ideas. They feel neglected and leave the church, taking their checkbooks with them. Soon after, John is fired.

Each of these stories has one thing in common: a failure of *contextual intelligence*.

Cynthia fell victim to a false assumption: what works in one context will work in all contexts. She played to her strengths, hitting the ground running with what worked in previous congregations. She didn't consider the aging nature of the congregation or the mass migration of folks from the neighborhood. Just before she arrived, the railroad, the major industry of this town, relocated further north. Now all families associated with the railroad have left town or are in an economic dilemma.

The once thriving denomination failed to understand the makeup of its own constituency and the voids between local congregations and communities. They focused on a handful of symptomatic problems while leaving the underlying causes of decline untreated. They defaulted to institutional strategies based on increasingly false assumptions. As if caught in a time capsule of irrelevancy, they are embroiled in a battle from which society has largely moved on. They hold to familiar ways of thinking and acting that blind them to changing contextual realities. The denominational structures are stuck in a regulatory mode and find it hard (and threatening) to transition from regulation to resource.

John trusted that his new congregation had an accurate assessment of their context. He also failed to understand that the way in which a congregation views their relationship with the community and the actuality of that relationship can be different. In his setting, the vision to bolster membership with young families was a setup for failure, being that the congregation sits on the edge of a retirement community.

Cynthia has a naturally high EQ (emotional intelligence). She knows how to love and lead people into health. But she did not consider the post-Christendom implications of her time, which has moved from *Leave It to Beaver* to *Beavis and Butt-Head* and *The Simpsons* to *Family Guy* and *Modern Family*. Whereas less than a lifetime ago, church and culture washed each other's hands, the culture has now washed its hands of the church and makes sure the church's dirty linens are aired in public. At best, going to church has all the appeal of a wet weekend. At worst, church is a scary place filled with horrifying people.

John showed high ability in one specific gifting but failed to understand his context and adapt his skills accordingly. The episcopal leaders lacked relational authority and credible scaffolding with the people under their care. Distracted with the presenting symptoms, they never dealt with the underlying causes of decline. They also failed to understand the macro context of a global denomination or the anti-institutional push against pyramidal hierarchies and the new protestant (in the true meaning of the word—to protest against), spiritual-but-not-religious Zeitgeist.

We believe that if these leaders knew Issachar's secret—the ancient secret to frontline mission—a totally different future may have been possible. We wrote this book so faithful church leaders can avoid mistakes like this and grow in CQ: *contextual intelligence*.

CHAPTER 2

WHO ARE THE ISSACHARIANS?

Of Issachar, those who had understanding of the times, to know what Israel ought to do, two hundred chiefs, and all their kindred under their command.

—1 Chronicles 12:32

In 1 Chronicles 12, the people are in a liminal space, a time between the times. Various constituencies of the tribes are rallying around David in the wilderness. While Saul is still technically king and David's movement is restricted, these supporters are of one mind to make David king. They are bringing support, in terms of people, power, wisdom, and resources. Thus, this is a time between two ages: the reign of Saul and the reign of David. The two paradigms exist simultaneously betwixt and between these kingships and their distinct ways of ordering society.

The tribe of Issachar shows up: the semioticians—sign readers—who "had understanding of the times" and an ability to "know what Israel ought to do." At the most basic level, semiotics refers to the study of signs and symbols

Each of the twelve tribes of Israel has a special gift, a special mission, a special symbol.

as elements of communicative behavior. When the tribe of Issachar pledges its support, there is almost a collective sigh of relief. Each of the twelve tribes of Israel has a special gift, a special mission, a special symbol. Issacharians are scholar-strategist-practitioners who offer a twofold contribution: a semiotic reading of Scripture and a high level of contextual intelligence. These are two indispensable gifts to the whole people of Israel.

First, Issacharians know best their own story and can read best the current placement of that story in new landscapes. Second, based on their ability to understand the times, they have an ability to "know what Israel ought to do." Issacharians know their world in light of the Word, and they know a path forward into the future God is calling them to enter.

The Issacharians are celebrated for their high CQ partly because they are comfortable living in the *withness* of *betweenness* and *midstness*. Issacharians live "between the sheepfolds" (Gen. 49:14). They are tent dwellers (Deut. 33:18) who dedicate themselves to the study of the Scriptures, learning the lay of the land and reading the signs of the times. Their contextual intelligence is oriented toward a hermeneutic and a semiotic together: interpreting the Scriptures (hermeneutic) and reading the signs of a specific context (semiotic). The following Venn diagram highlights the CQ sweet spot of the Issachar mandorla (an almond-shaped area that can be created by two overlapping circles).

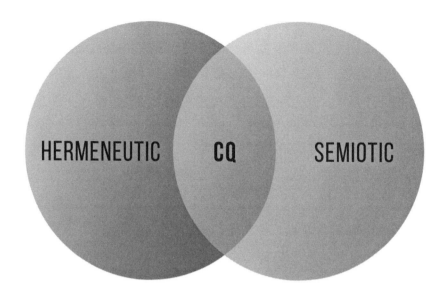

Figure 1: Issachar Mandorla

Because of the clarity and understanding they discern from those yoked levels of *withness*, Issacharians are consulted in mapping a plan of action ("knowing what to do"). Organizationally speaking, they are the strategists, future casters, and scenario thinkers of the community.

Perhaps the characteristics of this wisdom is embodied most clearly in Tola, the seventh judge of Israel:

> *After Abimelech, Tola son of Puah son of Dodo, a man of Issachar, who lived at Shamir in the hill country of Ephraim, rose to deliver Israel. He judged Israel twenty-three years. Then he died, and was buried at Shamir.*
>
> *—Judges 10:1–2*

In contrast to Abimelech's three-year reign of terror that preceded him (to which is devoted an entire chapter in Judges 9), the Bible devotes merely two short verses to this twenty-three-year reign of Tola. Nathan Moskowitz is a neurosurgeon, a professor at Johns Hopkins University, a Hebrew scholar, and an artist/painter of the story of Israel. In his commentaries, he has introduced what we call the "Moskowitz Rule": "Biblical brevity typically conveys epochal serenity."[1] The clues to Tola's life, he argues, are embedded in the meaning and symbolism of some names mentioned in these verses. He outlines a hypothetical reconstruction of Tola's judgeship by analyzing the names associated with him and by "juxtaposing them alongside the multiple biblical references and prophecies that refer to his tribal patriarch Issachar."[2]

Tola's genealogy is significant. He is described as "Tola son of Puah . . . who lived at Shamir." Each of these names mirrors the name of one of Issachar's sons: Tola, Puvah, Jashob, and Shimron (Gen. 46:13). Further, Tola's name and that of his father are virtually identical with the names of the first two sons of Issachar. The name of Tola's city, Shamir, is similar to Issachar's fourth son's name, Shimron. Moskowitz argues that these similarities are highlighted in the text to strengthen the connection between Tola and Issachar. This association of Tola with classical Issachar names presents Tola as "the embodiment of the blessings given to Issachar."[3]

The deathbed blessing of Jacob over his son Issachar goes like this:

> *Issachar is a strong donkey, lying down between the sheepfolds; he saw that a resting place was good, and that the land was pleasant; so he bowed his shoulder to the burden, and became a slave at forced labor.*
>
> —*Genesis 49:14–15*

Contained in the blessing of Issachar by his father Jacob are two major themes: peace and hard work. First, "lying down between the sheepfolds" is a geographical metaphor that conveys a feeling of domestic calm. Or in Moskowitz's words:

The domestication of the ass and sheep and the utilitarian production of wool all imply an atmosphere of serenity; of commerce rather than combat.

This would add to the idea of tranquility implied in the very brevity of the verses describing Tola's judgeship.[4]

The second pronounced theme in the blessing of Issachar is the "willingness to perform hard work: he bent his shoulder to the burden, and became a toiling serf."[5] What this suggests about Tola, Moskowitz infers, is that "he worked very hard as a leader and saw himself as a servant of the people, instead of demanding that the people serve him."[6]

What a marked contrast to the rule of Abimelech before him, who sought to master and rule over the people. The difference between Abimelech and Tola is the difference between two very distinct leadership styles: a positional/ hierarchal individualist approach (Abimelech) and a shared/adaptive relational approach (Tola). The great Ukrainian rabbi and biblical scholar Malbim (1809–1879) insists the text is contrasting Tola with Abimelech: "Abimelech sought to lord it over the Israelites as his subjects, whereas Tola sought to help them and take care of their needs."[7]

The domestic calm reveals a kind of peaceful disposition, while the willingness to serve *with*, not *over*, denotes a kind of deep humility. These two themes are expanded to include the wisdom of scholarship in Moses's blessing on the two tribes that are often tied together in the Scriptures—the entrepreneurial Zebuluns and the scholarly Issacharians: "And of Zebulun he said: 'Rejoice, O Zebulun, on your journeys, and Issachar, in your tents.'"[8]

The theme of domestic bliss and tranquility associated with Issachar is further advanced by the qualifier "enjoying life in his tent." Moskowitz helps us scratch under the surface a bit to get the deeper levels of meaning: "*In your tents* [be-ohalekha] are understood by the Sages to convey intellectuality by referring to the tents under which the Torah is studied."[9] The first place this concept appears is in Genesis in the distinction between Jacob, "a mild man who stayed in tents," and Esau, the skillful hunter who was "a man of the outdoors."[10]

Issachar and Zebulun, unlike most commonly paired sets of biblical brothers, do not become adversaries or even rivals. The tribe of Zebulun actually subsidizes Issachar (Deut. 33:18–19). They are most often *with* one another, to the point where one can't speak of one tribe without the other:

Issachar and Zebulun choose to work together, combining their separate and different skills to their mutual advantage. According to the Midrash, it was Zebulun who, as a merchant, went to sea in order to give both tribes financial support, whereas Issachar remained at home (in his tent), studying Torah, in order to give both tribes spiritual and intellectual uplift. [11]

We know this is a lot, but stay with us here. It will make more sense later when we suggest cultivating contextually intelligent teams of first-class noticers. Right now we are laying a biblical basis for CQ, the structural supports of strategic partnerships, shared leadership, and the theory of PALS (Pooling, Allying, Linking) [12] in the kind of effectual reasoning employed by successful entrepreneurs.

Issachar's "erudition and scholarly judgment" [13] must inform our reading of the key text of 1 Chronicles 12:32. Tola, a humble, peaceful judge of Israel for twenty-three years, symbolizes the essence of the Issacharians and embodies the "qualities of scholarship and learning that minimized any internal civil strife and which, through mediation, averted any potential external strife."[14] A final connection with Tola's father's name, Puah, is worthy of note. Midrash ha-Gadol associates the name Puah with that of a plant (madder) used to make dyes: "Just as *puah* colors everything, so does the tribe of Issachar cover the world with Torah."[15]

In sum, the Issacharians enjoy a competency in both the reading of sacred content and the reading of worldly context. This resonates with the organizational scenario thinking of experts in strategic management who highlight the importance of accurately perceiving and evaluating an environment, as well as moving from intellection to action or strategy delineation to implementation.[16]

When times are troubled and the transitions are uncertain, Issacharians are called upon in the liminality to "read the signs" (rightly perceive) as well as to "know what to do" (implement strategies). They see the overlap and yoke content and context, and like the donkey that is the symbol of the tribe, they bear the weight of showing how to move forward into the future.

In a pandemic world, now more than ever, we need contextually intelligent disciples to arise and lead local churches to flourish. This is our "Issachar moment" like never before. God has given all people the capacity to grow in contextual intelligence. In this book, we will lay out a framework, centered in the very mind of Christ (Phil. 2), and suggest a palette of competencies to help learn the ancient Issachar way for this newly emerging reality.

CHAPTER 3

WHAT IS CONTEXTUAL INTELLIGENCE?

"Take a lesson from the fig tree. From the moment you notice its buds form, the merest hint of green, you know summer's just around the corner. So it is with you: When you see all these things, you'll know he's at the door."

—Matthew 24:32–33, msg

Contextual intelligence is the ability to accurately diagnose a context and make the correct decisions regarding what to do.

Yale psychologist Robert Sternberg (1985) first popularized the term *contextual intelligence* in his contention that any intelligence must take place in an actual context and that its assessment must be contextually oriented.

The term *contextual intelligence* was later used by Penn State social scientist Patrick T. Terenzini (1993) in his award-winning research into educational institutions.[17] He proposed that there are three tiers of skills that are necessary for effective institutional research: technical knowledge (mastering technical skills), issues intelligence (defining problems and applying techniques from Tier 1), and contextual intelligence (understanding the historical, philosophical, and political realities, as well as the values, attitudes, and decision-making processes, which makes possible the practical application of technical and issues intelligence to an organizational context).[18]

Contextual intelligence (CQ) comes from the Latin root *contextere*, which means "to weave together," and the conjunction of two Latin words: *inter* (between) and *legere* (to choose or read). Matthew Kutz, an award-winning author, professor, Fulbright scholar, and leading researcher in the area of contextual intelligence, first described CQ as "accurately reading between the lines" (the threads that intertwine to form a context) and "making correct decisions regarding what to do." [19]

This is Issachar's secret, a distinct kind of intelligence embodied by the tribe of Issachar. In a time of great transition and change, they were able to accurately diagnose the context ("read the signs") and effectively apply their knowledge ("know what to do").

We will show clearly that the greatest example of this intelligence is embodied in the life of Jesus himself. We know this is a bit of a reach, but perhaps it's no mere coincidence that Jesus rides into Jerusalem on the very symbol of Issachar, a donkey, the humble domesticated beast of burden:

> *Rejoice greatly, Daughter Zion! Shout, Daughter Jerusalem! See, your king comes to you, righteous and victorious, lowly and riding on a donkey, on a colt, the foal of a donkey.*
> —*Zechariah 9:9, niv*

Each of the four Gospels showcase how Jesus strategically stages this activity to fulfill this prophecy (Matt. 21:1–11; Mark 11:1–11; Luke 19:28–44; John 12:12–19). As Jesus descends from the Mount of Olives toward Jerusalem and inserts himself into the Procession of the Lambs, the crowds lay their clothes on the ground to welcome him as he, the true Paschal Lamb that will take away the sins of the world, peacefully enters Jerusalem. The Procession of the Lambs from Bethlehem to Jerusalem, where hundreds of lambs are led through the Lamb's Gate for Passover sacrifice, is a kind of anti-power parade, an inverted spectacle from the triumphal military entry of the Caesars. Anyone familiar with the Hebrew religion would be able to make connections with Jesus's many layers of symbolic activity as he presents himself on that donkey.

Further, there are many similarities in the dispositions of Jesus, Tola, and the Issacharians. Jesus is not an Abimelech type of leader but of the character of Tola. He is not a Caesar, thundering into the city on a war horse with legions of military units in his wake. The sign of the donkey speaks loudly on this. The so-called Palm Sunday "triumphal entry" also signifies the full inauguration of the greatest transition in human history. The life, death, and resurrection of Jesus of Nazareth was a cosmic movement from the "age of the law" to the "age of faith" (Rom. 10:4). This launches the in-betweenness of Israel to New Israel and the grafting in of the Gentiles into the family of God. The whole New Testament takes place amid this shift of ages "betwixt and between" one reality and into another, from Torah True expressed as text and law to Torah True embodied as person and love.

> *The so-called Palm Sunday "triumphal entry" also signifies the full inauguration of the greatest transition in human history.*

Jesus's life and ministry initiate this transformation, but the rest of the New Testament is formed in response. The story of the early church is the story of the first disciples unlearning, improvising, and responding to these implications. What is more, Jesus is the greatest manifestation of intelligence ever possessed by a single person. While this intelligence has many facets, one dimension of this intelligence is contextual intelligence. This is true on multiple levels, as we will show:

1) The incarnation is a manifestation of contextual intelligence.

2) Jesus teaches his disciples how to grow in their contextual intelligence.

3) Jesus bequeaths the church with his own contextual intelligence, the "mind of Christ" (Phil. 2:1–11).

We want to invite you to consider that the highest form of intelligence is not analytic intelligence (IQ, or intelligence quotient, involving information-processing abilities), emotional intelligence (EQ, or emotional quotient, using emotional information to guide thinking and behavior), relational intelligence (RQ, or relational quotient, an umbrella term for emotional intelligence, social intelligence, and relational dynamics between people), or even cultural intelligence (the other CQ, or cultural quotient, refers to the capability to interact across cultures), but rather contextual intelligence (CI), which again is the ability to read the signs and know what to do.

Contextual intelligence is a servant of all other forms of intelligence. Cultivating a high contextual intelligence quotient (CQ) involves growing in the ability to read the complex threads (geographic, temporal, cultural, economic, organizational, emotional, political, and so on) of a context and adapt information appropriately for that environment to solve specific challenges and create a flourishing future.

Vincent Donovan was a Roman Catholic missionary to the Masai people in Tanzania for almost two decades. He discovered many of the assumptions

18

he learned in his training were false and that the conventional missionary methods were not transferable in the context of the collectivistic tribal culture of the Masai. He found the highly individualized Western approach of evangelizing people one by one to be ineffective, and he began to question the whole missionary system.

Becoming aware that his context needed to dictate his missional approach, Donovan wrote a letter to his bishop requesting "a radical departure from the traditional procedure." Donovan started with what he calls a "cleansing of the mind," or what we will refer to as *unlearning*. He then immersed himself in the culture of the Masai and began to ask them, "Who is God to you?" He constructed bridges of meaning starting on their side of the shore. Only then could he plant the seeds of the gospel "in the Masai culture, and let it grow wild."

Donovan wrote:

An evangelist, a missionary must respect the culture of a people, not destroy it. The incarnation of the gospel, the flesh and blood which must grow on the gospel is up to the people of a culture...[20]

Vincent Donovan shows us what contextual intelligence looks like in practice. He "read the signs" of a time and culture and discerned "what to do" as the appropriate course of action. The result was the embodiment of new, contextually appropriate forms of church.

Let us return to Cynthia, our pastor friend we introduced in the beginning. One of her practices at previous revitalizations is what she termed "winning the LOLs" (an acronym for little old ladies). By visiting the matriarchs of congregations in their homes, she was doing what we term in the field of contextual intelligence "joining through the hierarchy." If church leaders want to have kingdom impact, we need to join and enlist the support of those at the top of the hierarchy, and in Cynthia's case, these were indeed the LOLs.

What she did not consider was that in previous congregations, she followed clergy who were simply neglectful of the needs of the congregants. When she came along, showing genuine care for the spiritual matriarchs, many people who had left the congregations returned. She was entering into what we will describe in detail later as a *kind learning environment*, in which consistent outcomes are linked directly to the appropriate actions.

In her new appointment, this was not the case. The aging nature of the congregation and the mass migration of folks from the neighborhood due to the railroad's relocation created a *wicked learning environment*, in which the link between outcome and actions is misleading. No amount of targeted care for the inherited congregation could have produced revitalization. The previous membership had moved away, leaving only families with no previous connection to the church who were experiencing an economic dilemma. Cynthia was operating in a *closed system*, in which a system's operations do not depend on the context.

Later, we will describe *3D thinking*, which is "doing time" by utilizing hindsight, insight, and foresight.[21] Let us employ hindsight in Cynthia's situation and imagine she made one small CQ adaptation. In addition to all her usual strategies, she informed the congregation that she would move her normal Monday office hours to the local diner from nine in the morning until noon. By immersing herself in the context, she connected with some of the servers. These were the "persons of peace" (Luke 10:6) in this community. They knew everybody in the town (and everybody's business) through their work. They gave relational access to networks of individuals outside the life of the church. Furthermore, as Cynthia formed relationships with the servers, she learned about their struggles. She became a pastor to them. They began to attend worship on Sunday mornings, and they brought friends—lots of them! Over time, revitalization occurred in a contextually appropriate way.

A failure of CQ can occur at any level of organization and have far-reaching consequences. The once thriving global denomination now on the verge of schism failed to develop contextual maps and provided no framework to harvest learning at every level of the organization. Information seemed to only flow downward, from the top of a pyramidal structure, far removed from the daily challenges of local churches.

This played into unfortunate existing stereotypes about an institutional elite who themselves risk no personal exposure but exert tremendous control—the leaders at the center of a power hub who have become entirely out of touch with local realities while still making decisions for them. They defaulted to an intervention strategy that included a small group of episcopal leaders (the formal power) who handpicked a working party to make decisions for the entire organization—heroes of the hierarchy who would roll out the perfect "save the denomination" plan, if you will. They underestimated the disposition of the people they were charged to care for: the local congregations (the informal power). They failed to understand the nature of grassroots alliances with very deep and opposing theological convictions.

Because they operated in a rigid hierarchy, which saw their role as regulatory in nature, they failed to understand the need to resource congregations to faithfully adapt to their multitude of diverse contexts. Had they been flexible and created ways for situation-specific learning to enter at every level of the organization, they may have countered these powerful institutional attitudes. Rather, they diverted to a linear power model, the vestige of a Constantinian iteration of the church. This was an inappropriate means of influence in an anti-institutional, post-hierarchical, network, and polycentric societal context.

They defaulted to a technical problem/solution scenario rather than preparing for an adaptive challenge. They merely addressed presenting symptoms and not the underlying causes and conditions of decline. They avoided treating the real factors that stunted vitality, including professionalization of the clergy, loss of the small-group system, the diminishment of equipping laity for mission, and the institutional voids between franchise-like local congregations and the rapidly changing communities that cradle their life.

CHAPTER 4

WHY CONTEXTUAL INTELLIGENCE?

"When it is evening, you say, 'It will be fair weather, for the sky is red.'
And in the morning, 'It will be stormy today, for the sky is red and
threatening.' You know how to interpret the appearance of the sky, but
you cannot interpret the signs of the times."

—Matthew 16:2–3

The first thing George Washington (1732–1799) did after becoming president was to take a trip through all thirteen states. He wanted to contextualize in his mind and heart the whole of this new nation. But to make sure no one took his presidential journey to be some royal procession, he refused to stay in the elegant houses of the local rich. Instead, he sheltered in lodging and inns available to every traveler. Now the signage of "George Washington stayed here" marks the journey. Hence, the tradition of tracking the tracks of George Washington in that first trip across America.[22]

This was a time of tremendous change and revolution, and perhaps there is something we can learn from Washington. Christians are people who are tracking through the colonies of heaven and earth. We are trailing the tracks of the Trinity in our particular contexts.

The church in the twenty-first century is also in an age of great transition. We have both written at length about these changes—Len most recently in *Rings of Fire: Walking in Faith Through a Volcanic Future*, and Michael most recently in *A Field Guide to Methodist Fresh Expressions* and the *Deep Roots, Wild Branches* series. In this current work, we move beyond "reading the signs" and more fully into "knowing what to do."

So many voices join in the death-dealing chorus that perpetuates a song of decline and church closure. The great challenge of reChristianizing a post-Christendom world dominates the ecclesial conversation in the West. Be that as it may, here we want to hum a new tune and joyfully proclaim that we find ourselves on the edge of the greatest missional opportunity in the history of the West. Let's change the song.

We live in a world where the context can change in a second. Some contexts change after the change sneaks up on us like a frog in a slowly boiling pot. But some contexts can change overnight. The sudden appearance of black swans, 800-pound gorillas, dropping dinosaurs, runaway trains, wild cards, or a house of cards can usher in a new reality that requires a new normality.[23]

As we've learned from COVID-19, the first global black swan, one virus can change the face and future of the world; and the church. One crisis virus did to clericalism in the Catholic Church what two thousand years of reformation could not. One global lockdown did to the resistance to installing an Internet front door in every church what two decades of books and lectures and seminars failed to do.[24]

A post-COVID world requires the church to read the Story again from a new vantage point, not so we can stockpile and be selfish but so we can reach out to others in healing, kindness, and service. When contexts change, the church must be prepared to fast-forward the future, which is often found in a harkening back and a taking back of the past from a backslidden present.

The "problem" is not only that the church now finds herself positioned on the geothermic ticking time bomb of a super volcano of change. It's how she thinks about and responds to that change. Western churches have a thinking problem—a reduced way of understanding God, creation, other human beings, and the larger communal ecosystems that cradle the life of inherited congregations. Contextual intelligence offers us a way to be absorbed into the mind of Christ and turn the energy of those shifts into opportunities.

Contextual intelligence offers us a way to be absorbed into the mind of Christ and turn the energy of those shifts into opportunities.

Two researchers and respected professors at Harvard, Anthony J. Mayo and Nitin Nohria, conducted a massive study of the thousand most influential business leaders of the twentieth century. They termed this group "the canon of business legends."[25] They found that there was great variety in traits, such as charismatic personalities, analytical intelligence, creativity, and low risk aversion. The only commonality that tied them together was the application of their unique set of strengths within differing contextual settings. Mayo and Nohria called this *contextual intelligence* and defined it as "the profound sensitivity to macro-level contextual factors in the creation, growth, or transformation of businesses."[26]

What makes a successful organization, then, is the ability of that organization to make sense of the spirit of the times and to harness the opportunities it presents. The best leaders appreciate and understand their situation in the world. They also lead teams with an innate consciousness of their contexts, with an understanding of the level of change, and by responding in ways that capitalize on the opportunities embedded in the emerging challenges. Contextual intelligence is increasingly seen as more essential than IQ and more predictive than EQ because of the decline of the "great man theory" and the rise of teams of "first-class noticers."[27]

What enabled these leaders to be successful in their time when so many others failed? According to Mayo and Nohria, it was contextual intelligence.

The church is filled with clergy who do well what they were trained and programmed to do in seminary. Yet they are ill prepared to pay attention to their context or to integrate into their visualization of the future the massive changes taking place in their context and community. Many apply successful tactics ("best practices") from previous appointments of decades past with little sensitivity to variations of context and chronology. Lavish dreams aren't built on sparse knowledge of one's neighborhood or neighbors. Think about our friend Cynthia, who may have triggered revitalization by immersing herself in the context and getting to know the natives.

Many churches don't know their communities, and their communities don't know them. Pastors are largely caring for the dwindling numbers of faithful but fidgety, feisty, and fearful church members, and they are often overwhelmed by the infighting that comes from facing inward, not outward, with little connection to the greater community. Remember our pastor friend John from the opening stories, who assumed his new congregation had an accurate assessment of their community? He was unaware that their visioning process never considered the contextual factors cradling the congregation's very life. The vision of a young-family revival in a retirement community may sound absurd, except that this is a real story from one of our ministries, as all three opening vignettes are.

Fortunately, Mayo's and Nohria's research makes clear that contextual intelligence is not possessed by one type of person, such as the edgy and creative entrepreneur who is often screened out of the ordination process, but also by stabilizers, managers, and leaders across the board.

Emerging research in cognitive neuroscience is helping us understand how the brain pays attention. This is an acquired skill that one can practice and grow in one's proficiency. Unlearning, listening, paying attention, and semiotics skill sets for various contexts can be taught and enhanced. The disconnect between awareness and action highlights the distinct challenges of both reading a context accurately and knowing what to do.

Harvard professor Tarun Khanna, who specializes in entrepreneurship in emerging markets, defines *contextual intelligence* for the corporate context as "the ability to understand the limits of our knowledge, and to adapt that knowledge to a context different from the one in which it was developed."[28] Many corporations cling to what Peter Senge calls *mental models* that blind them to contextual variation. They are committed to "deeply held internal images of how the world works," often learned in school and just as often unconscious, "images that limit us to familiar ways of thinking and acting."[29]

Khanna coins the term *institutional voids* to describe the absence of intermediaries like market research firms and credit card systems to efficiently connect buyers and sellers in emerging markets.[30] Quite simply, these voids occur when the institutional scaffolding that supports the market (or the church) are absent, weak, or fail to fulfill their roles. Khanna shows that contextually intelligent leaders turn the challenges of these voids into opportunities for entrepreneurship and business growth.

For a variety of reasons, local churches have adopted short-sighted shortcuts and faulty mental models that obstruct their contexts and blind them to the institutional voids that block their mission. Contextually intelligent pioneers see these voids as opportunities for social innovation. They hypothesize alternative mental models, which prompt the creation of needed relational scaffolding throughout the community. This can birth new kinds of contextual churches, ones that can even be tethered to existing institutions and structures.

A crude analogy to explain an institutional void? Let's say you want to start a Chick-fil-A franchise in a remote desert among a group of indigenous tribes. Once your building is constructed, you discover there is no supply chain infrastructure, no electric power grid, no Wi-Fi or telecommunication networks. Furthermore, these indigenous peoples consider chicken a sacred animal that cannot be harmed under threat of execution.

Where do you find yourself? With no credibility enhancers, no information analyzers and advisors, no aggregators and distributors, and so on. All this, in addition to a product you cannot sell. While hyperbolic, this is the situation many churches find themselves in. Our default setting is to sit down and eat our own product until it's gone. Then we eat the seed corn until there is none left. Then we close the church.

Contextual intelligence demands a mental model that anticipates contextual fluctuations and variance. We find out what the tribes actually eat (something we learn from eating with them), we recode and reframe our communications accordingly, we build the necessary networks, and we repurpose the space in a contextually appropriate way.

In this time that's been coined *post-Christendom*, the *Great Decline*, and the *Post-Christian United States*, how are some church leaders succeeding where so many others are failing? Contextual intelligence.

In the ecclesial realm, local churches are stuck in brittle mental models that blind us to changing contextual realities. The phenomenon of institutional voids plays out in local churches that try to franchise one version of church with no contextual sensitivity. The voids describe the lack of awareness and the absence of scaffolding that can connect churches with their communities. Also lacking is a viable framework to do so. While all intelligences are needed on the new missional frontier, the cultivation of contextual intelligence can weave them all together, bridge the gaps, and help us adapt to the emerging opportunities. In fact, CQ is the one intelligence to serve all the multiple intelligences.

Singaporean law-partner-turned-preacher and Bible teacher T C Choong identifies the "divine and unique framework" of Jesus's intelligence as contextual intelligence and refers to it as "the golden thread" of all Jesus's interactions with people and the open sesame to his messiahship.[31] Long before contextual intelligence became the shibboleth of management, scientists, and corporate consultants, Jesus taught the disciples to learn from and situate themselves in their surroundings—to look, observe, consider, behold, watch, and respond (Matt. 6:26–29). We will follow the golden thread of Jesus's own intelligence to suggest a framework for the cultivation of a higher CQ.

The modern project is collapsing. Something new is struggling to be born. The current Constantinian attractional mode of the church is a mental model not connecting with a culture of four types of religious sensibility: nones, dones, somes, and comes. The fastest-growing segment of the population are nones and dones—those who say they have no religious affiliation or those who say "been there, done that, no more." The number of somes (those who identify with a religion but only attend sporadically) and comes (the faithful) are diminishing faster than anyone wants to admit. Increasingly, we are finding ourselves in a Judges 2:10 situation:

Moreover, that whole generation was gathered to their ancestors, and another generation grew up after them, who did not know the Lord or the work that he had done for Israel.

It is not just that we live in a world that has banished the gods but not the devils. We live in a world that has made gods of the devils. In times like these, times of subversive transition and revolutionary change, the contextual intelligence of the Issachar tribe is needed more than ever. But beware—Issacharians bring heart-rending, mind-bending, spine-chilling, soul-stirring wisdom. This book calls for a new Order of Issachar—students of the Word in connection with the world, and strategists for the future.

Jesus expects contextually intelligent disciples today. "You know how to read the signs of the sky," Jesus said. "You must also learn how to read the signs of the times" (Matt. 16:3). These words define the mission of the tribe of Issachar, those who were the best scholars of Scripture but who also were the best at "understanding the times, and knowing what Israel ought to do."

We are calling for this new Order of Issachar to arise—Issacharians who can read the shifts in the sands of time but know, like the ancient twelve tribes of Israel on pilgrimage did, that while we live in changing contexts, there is always an unchanging home. It is time for the church to heed Jesus's call to be contextually intelligent, to find the God stance in every circumstance. This is the ancient secret to frontline mission.

CHAPTER 5

WELCOME TO THE STUDIO

I look both to art history and to vision studies to think about the
relationship between attention and volition—how we might not only
disentangle ourselves from the attention economy but learn to wield
attention in a more intentional way.

—Jenny Odell,

artist, writer, and professor at Stanford University[32]

Here's a bit on how to read this book.

We want you to treat it the way an artist treats a studio. A *studio* is a
generic term for the workroom of an artist and team of apprentices. It
can be a space for collaborative architecture, painting, pottery, origami,
woodworking, scrapbooking, music making, photography, film production,
sermon preparation, and the list goes on. Jesus is described as inheriting
from Joseph, his father, the trade of a τέκτων (*tektōn*). This word is often
translated *carpenter* or *mason* but can just as easily be translated, and perhaps
more accurately, as *craftsman* or *artisan* or *architect*. It can also refer to an

31

artist, including the art of poetry; a maker of songs; a strategist; or a scholar-writer.

Jesus possessed the greatest contextual intelligence in the history of the universe. He was contextual intelligence *incarnate*. Jesus most certainly learned at home and studied at the local synagogue. He learned Hebrew, Aramaic, and Greek, and he studied the written Torah, the highest form of worship, tediously memorizing, repeating, and reciting. He even mastered the emerging cutting-edge technologies of his day, which only a very small percentage of the population were proficient in—reading and writing. Yet his imagination, teaching, and parables were most reflective of an artist or a gardener. Jesus's art was a life lived and words spoken with an astonishingly lucid, very local, contextualized expression of God's eternal truth.

It was the Hungarian-British chemist and philosopher Michael Polanyi (1891–1976) who first challenged the notion of objectivity and wrote most persuasively that knowing is really more of an art, in which the knower is always guided by their passion, personal commitment, and underlying assumptions. In introducing the concept of *post-critical* to the modern Enlightenment world of science and technology, Polanyi wrote:

> *To hold such knowledge is an act deeply committed to the conviction that there is something there to be discovered. It is personal, in the sense of involving the personality of him who holds it, and also in the sense of being, as a rule, solitary; but there is no trace in it of self-indulgence. The discoverer is filled with a compelling sense of responsibility for the pursuit of a hidden truth, which demands his services for revealing it. His act of knowing exercises a personal judgement in relating evidence to an external reality, an aspect of which he is seeking to apprehend.*[33]

There is no pure, objective theology, nor is there such a church—pure, objective, ideal. There is only a contextual knowing, a contextual theology, a contextual church, and a contextual intelligence. Intelligence does not develop in a vacuum or in a laboratory with standardized tests and objective answers.

We first discovered the word *excelerate* in spray-painted graffiti. *Excelerate* is a mashup of two words: *excel* and *accelerate*. When you develop proficiency at something quickly and exceed all expectations, you excelerate. Exceleration of your CQ is our hope for your team as you invest time in this studio and take Issachar's secret into the world.

Contextual intelligence involves slowing down, reading details, connecting dots, and scanning the writing on the wall of local contexts. This is something both individuals and churches are struggling to do these days.

My (Michael) eleven-year-old daughter, Angel, is currently doing "textual evidence" exercises for homework. She is instructed to read the text, pause, read it again, and answer questions. Some of the answers can only be induced by tending details in the context. She is learning a CQ practice in her sixth-grade reading class. We have purposely designed sections of this book to be read in this way. We know this is countercultural in a world where our attention spans have been diminished and you must communicate in tweets to be heard. The text itself is an exercise in some of the skills we will suggest later. Learning focused attention skills in this studio will excelerate your contextual intelligence quotient (CQ).

Further, developing a high CQ is more an art than a science. Art requires us to employ the focus of attention in different ways and degrees. Contextual intelligence is less about crunching the data (infographics, demographics, and psychographics) about a context and more about immersion in, and relationships with the people in, that context. It's also a collaborative art form. The most potent intelligence is a *collective intelligence*—that's why we invite you to excelerate your CQ by co-creating with your team. What we offer you here is an artist studio, a space to grab some brushes and sling some kingdom paint around in your community, to see and showcase for others the epic beauty, goodness, and truth that's already baked in to your context at every level but is sometimes hidden.

The school of painting known as realism is about capturing the movement, light, and details of a person or scene as accurately as possible. It is the style of representing familiar things as they actually are (often contrasted with idealism). Contextual intelligence involves learning to understand and form an accurate picture of a context as it really is, while at the same time recognizing that just as scenes from real life move and change as soon as we capture them, so does a context.

Once that accurate portrait of the context as it is in that moment is painted, then we can create new dimensions and new dreams. We can see the gaps, the things that are, the things that need to be, and the things that are yet to be. We can contribute meaningfully to the context by honoring it, understanding it, engaging it as it actually is, and moving it forward into the future.

All master artists start by learning the fundamentals of their art. We must do the same, learning how to hold the brush and how a stroke and a canvas meet. We learn our colors, how they mix and blend and complement each other. We learn how to draw lines, shade, fill, and so on. Master artists start with simple beginnings. This is true of growing in our contextual intelligence as well.

So, rather than a table of contents, chapters, and series of "logues" (prologues, monologues, and epilogues), we invite you to our studio to take the contents on the table and co-create with your team.

Opening Images. Every studio has pieces hanging around for inspiration.

Here we present two of them that demonstrate contextual intelligence to jumpstart your creative juices.

Priming the Canvas. Artists can prime their canvas by applying a layer or two of gesso to the surface. This helps the colors pop. When painting with oil color, if the canvas is poorly primed, the oil may sink into the canvas, leaving blotches on the surface later. We want to prime your mental canvas with a brief contextualization of our own. Here we ground contextual intelligence in a theology of incarnation.

Contextual Intelligence Mandorla Ring. To simplify the process of contextualization, we use a symbol of two overlapping circles that birth a third, almond-shaped ring called a mandorla. The mandorla ring can be laid over any context to help us see the sweet spot of contextual ministry in a given location.

Contextual Intelligence Framework. Neither of us is quite fond of formulas or protocols that teach you "seven simple steps" or "how you can build a tower of Babel too!" Rather, we suggest in its place a mindset, a frame of mind, or a spiritcraft, a Spirit-driven armature of practices, postures, and pacts. We think of this as a series of triggers and trajectories through which our creativity flows. It's the bare frame on which we can hang our thoughts, a Situation Room where we can scheme and dream. We are not building from scratch. God has provided the undergirding structure. This framework is quite literally the incarnation of Jesus, outlined as the mind of Christ in Philippians 2:1–11 and informed by Ephesians 4 and the Gospels.

Palette of FYSAs. The intelligence community deploys an acronym that goes beyond FYI (For Your Information) to something equally as important: FYSA (For Your Situational Awareness). Think of this journey as your team boarding a train together. The contextual intelligence framework serves as a set of train tracks that will move through each of the FYSA competencies like a sequence of stations. Your team can stop at each station, survey what is offered, and take what's applicable to your context. In our experience, the contextual intelligence cultivation process usually happens through this series of moves. However, it's possible that different teams could start at different stations. These FYSAs will introduce the palette of competencies we will explore to help excelerate your CQ.

The Finishing Touch. Artists of every variety are always trying to master the perfect finish. The final note, coat, brushstroke, or detail—a "pop" that doesn't leave the beholder with a sense of closure but calls us deeper into a journey of mystery. Rather than a conclusion, we invite you to ponder the *holy hum*, the universal that resonates through every particular.

CHAPTER 6

OPENING IMAGES
The Power of Contextualization

Followers of Jesus must have insight into things spiritual. They must
be able to see the mountains filled with the horses and chariots of fire;
they must be able to interpret that which is written by the finger of
God upon the walls of conscience; they must be able to translate the
signs of the times into terms of their spiritual meaning: they must be
able to draw aside, now and then, the curtain of things material and
let mortals glimpse the spiritual glories which crown the mercy seat of
God. Followers of Jesus must declare the pattern that was shown him
on the mount; they must utter the vision granted to Jesus upon the isle
of revelation . . . None of these things can anyone do without spiritual
insight.

—Powhatan Wright James (1880–1956)[34]

Here in our studio, there are two pieces of art hanging on two walls,
opposite each other. We want you to pause and reflect upon them with us.
Let's read, evaluate, and interpret them together. Perhaps get your team to

spend some time silently perceiving them. What signs and symbols emerge for you? What pricks your soul? Does anything elicit an emotional reaction? What grabs you? After looking for a while, do you notice anything you didn't see at first?

We invite you not to just glimpse and move through to the next section. Let's stop, pay attention, and then read the reflection. We are preparing ourselves for the kind of seeing we will explore more fully later.

1) Altarpiece at St. Michael and All Angels, Bishop's Cleeve, Gloucestershire[35]

To celebrate the 950th anniversary of the church St. Michael and All Angels, in Bishop's Cleeve, Gloucestershire, the artist PJ Crook painted this triptych altarpiece, "Madonna of the Butterflies with Saints Michael and Jerome." It reveals a young Mary facing into the future while butterflies (symbols of resurrection) dance around her head and a caterpillar winds it way along the rail at the bottom.

The threefold-paneled painting was dedicated December 13, 2018, by Bishop Rachel Treweek. The left-hand panel shows St. Michael holding a cross entwined by a serpent, both showcasing the devil that St. Michael slew and the universal symbol for medicine. Behind him, in miniature, is the church in which the altarpiece stands. On the right, we see St. Jerome, translator of the Bible, accompanied by a lion—the sleepy lion from whose paw he removed the thorn. Behind are scenes of the flight into Egypt and the Sermon on the Mount. When the doors are closed, the figure of Christ praying in the garden is unveiled. The disciples are asleep in the corner, of course, while Judas leads a posse of men to arrest him. Note the lamb peering at you over the railing. The very Lamb of God who takes away the sins of the world is also the very Lion of the tribe of Judah.

Altarpieces often included some local figures highlighting the specific province of the painting and proving the provenance of its composition. Artists like Crook are masters at weaving contextuality and universality together. For example, emerging through the left-hand doorway of the central panel is a nurse, about to minister to the baby Jesus. This is a portrait of the artist's friend Margaret Whitehead, a school nurse, who was killed in a car accident.

Reflection Questions

- Does understanding the context of the painting change how you see it now? If so, in what ways?

- Can you think of any distinct contexual symbols unique to your own community?

- Who are the local saints stepping into the Jesus story in your congregation?

- In what ways is your church a weaving together of contextuality and universality?

2) Leonardo da Vinci's *The Last Supper*[36]

Before you is one of the most iconic pieces of Christian art in existence. Look at the painting as if for the first time. Do you notice anything unique or strange? First, someone put a door in the wall underneath Jesus and took out part of the table and his feet. This decision to cut away part of the painting and put in a door is of such immense stupidity, a true idiom of idiocy, that it deserves an annual tongue-in-cheek award named for it: the Duh Vinci Award. It would be similar to the Darwin Awards, which since 1985 have recognized those individuals who have contributed to human betterment by either taking themselves out of the gene pool or doing something so stupid it reminds us of how fragile that gene pool really is. The Duh Vinci Award would honor those individuals and churches who make decisions based on prudence and expedience and efficiency while missing the larger picture (in this case, defacing one of the treasures of the Western world).

The second thing that pops out at us very quickly is that all the disciples are seated on the same side of the table. This makes it look like da Vinci may have painted the fifteenth-century equivalent of a selfie, where everyone lines up for a photo shoot. No one gathers around a table on one side looking out, of course. Nor was the Upper Room table a long picnic table with benches but rather a triclinium table, a U-shaped table where everyone was facing each other.

Only in context does *The Last Supper* make sense and come alive. Here is the painting contextualized: Dominicans did not take a vow of silence, but they observed times of strict silence, especially at meals. They began the meal by washing their hands (the only part of their body they washed) and then knelt before a crucifix or crucifixion scene on the back wall, under which sat the prior observing the meal. All meals were communal meals, and the food from the monastery kitchen was notoriously bad, as painters who worked on the walls of refectories complained in their diaries throughout history.

During the meal, the prior would often authorize one monk to mount a reading chair and read from either the Bible or the writings of another Dominican (e.g., *The Golden Legend*). Even the Trappists, with their strict vow of silence, were known to select one amongst them for the midday refectory reading of either the Bible or some writing by another Trappist. The monks and sisters also could meditate on the paintings on the wall, most of which were food paintings from the Jesus story. The most common of these food images were Last Supper paintings, referred to collectively as *cenacoli* since these Last Supper paintings were specifically located in the convent refectories (where meals were taken), called *cenacoli* in Italian (*cenacolo*, singular). Even today, Florence is known as the worldwide "Capital of the *Cenacoli*."

Ludovico Sforza commissioned in late 1494 such a *cenacoli* for the refectory of Santa Maria della Grazie[37], although Sforza's first thought was to have *The Last Supper* provide an object for meditation in the Sforza family mausoleum.

Sforza himself joined the monks every Tuesday and Saturday for a meal. In other words, when you see a reproduction of *The Last Supper*, you are looking at a fresco on the front wall of a refectory where the monks ate. The back wall featured a crucifixion fresco by Giovanni Donato da Montorfano, to which Leonardo added figures of the Sforza family in tempera. Leonardo's mentor, Verrocchio, had never done a fresco. Leonardo had never done a fresco. Yet he had the confidence to undertake a huge project in a medium he'd never done before and in a size he'd never undertaken—the north wall of the refectory, a painting twenty-nine feet high (though now shortened by the cutout).

So, Da Vinci's *Last Supper* should be seen as a head table in a banquet hall of tables. When the monks gathered to eat together, they were sitting in a line of succession that started with Jesus and his disciples, continuing to the present day with them sustaining at every meal the traditions that Jesus had started.

Reflection Questions

- Does understanding the context of the painting change how you see it now? If so, in what ways?

- Can you think of symbols unique to your context that can only be fully understood from a local perspective?

- Is there a Duh Vinci Award moment in the history of your congregation, when you made a decision based on prudence, expedience, and efficiency while doing damage to the bigger picture of your mission?

- In what ways does your community misinterpret traditions of your church as a selfie while misunderstanding its contextually appropriate expression for a particular time?

- How might you reinterpret those misunderstood traditions for your context?

We hope these paintings demonstrate the power of contextualization. For instance, among other things, the altarpiece at St. Michael and All Angels demonstrates the importance of particularity in trying to communicate universality. Da Vinci's *The Last Supper* teaches us we can sacrifice the beauty of incarnation for the sake of our Western impulse of efficiency. Both show us the gaps in our own perceptions, which only context can rightly fill. In this book, you'll learn how to avoid the problem of seeing from a skewed mental model by doing the work of paying attention to context. The next section will be an exercise in minding the textual evidence. Get ready!

CHAPTER 7

PRIMING THE CANVAS

Humans have a responsibility to find themselves where they are, in their own proper time and place, in the history to which they belong and to which they must inevitably contribute either their response or their evasions, either truth and act, or mere slogan and gesture.

—Thomas Merton

Earlier we referenced how master painters prime their canvas. While methods vary among artists, typically after cleaning and stretching the canvas, a layer or two of gesso (a combination of oil with an inert white pigment, such as chalk, whiting, or plaster of Paris; and a binder, such as animal glue) is applied to the surface. This prework protects the canvas from deterioration, and the layer of primer helps bring out the colors in a more pronounced way. Applying gesso in thin coats ensures an even painting surface and creates a smooth finish, determining the final texture of a painting. Proper priming can minimize problems on the surface later.

We want to prime your soul canvas with the gesso of a *theology of the incarnation*. Contextual intelligence is grounded in the central affirmation that Jesus Christ, the second person of the Trinity, "was made flesh."

We share a dream for you and for your church. Our passion is for you to be a high CQ follower of Jesus. We have written this book to help raise the CQ (contextual intelligent quotient) of you and your church so that you can recognize God's thumbprint, track Jesus's footsteps, and feel the Spirit's breeze and blaze in the particular context to which God has called you.[38]

For us, Jesus of Nazareth, the historic person, fully human and fully God man, is "the gospel" (good news). Jesus himself is living word, incarnate, or "good news," contextualized in a specific place and among specific persons.

A gospel that is not contextualized is not faithful to the gospel.

Contextualization is the embodied expression and extension of incarnation. The Word Became Flesh, Incarnation, is the ultimate contextual intelligence. Contextual intelligence is all about incarnation. If we have a limited understanding of incarnation, we can never paint an accurate portrait of our context. Our perception will be blotchy and skewed at best.

In one of our opening stories, our friend Pastor John received a call to serve a congregation where he would be responsible to attract young families. The elder board's understanding of the larger community was drawn from past memories. Because they had not prayerfully immersed themselves in the context, they were unaware of the magnitude of the shifting age demographic. Their vision was fabricated in a church board room, rather than through time spent as an incarnational presence in the community.

A church that is not a contextualized expression of its community is not faithful to the gospel.

The incarnate Son of God, whose glory shines in the whole of creation, has a birth story that is steeped in the particular. Jesus was born at a particular time, in a particular place, to a particular couple, with a particular ancestry, who lived out a particular heritage from Adam through Abraham-Isaac-and-Jacob. The whole weight of the world rested on the whisper of one particular "Yes!" to God's request by one particular accomplice named Mary, whose crux, credence, and song altered the course of history.

The gospel is all about *placefulness*. Jenny Odell employs this term to describe sensitivity and responsibility to the historical (what happened here) and ecological (who and what lives, or lived, here). Odell holds up bioregionalism (this involves the interrelation of human activity with ecological and geographical features) as a model for how we might be able to think about our place again.[39] Places are not just merely physical space holders; they are living, breathing ecosystems. Places have a distinct web of relationships. Places are made of particular flowers, birds, insects, water sources, temperatures, climates, and mammals. When human beings are part of those ecosystems, the ecosystems include webs of customs, languages, cultures, and meaning systems.

> *Places are not just merely physical space holders; they are living, breathing ecosystems.*

Every place has a soundtrack. Jesus joined his life to the tune of a particular melody in a town called Nazareth. CQ is about hearing the soundtrack of our place and joining our lives to the song.

But all that particularity is there to tell a universal story. The story of that One is the story of us all. The story of the Incarnate One is the story of us, incarnations all. The story of the Son of God is the story of every son and daughter of God. The story of the Last Adam is the story of every descendant of the First Adam. The fundamental rule of contextuality is cross-eyed: the needle-eye particular is the way to the wide-eye universal. Every particular note belongs to a larger symphony.

Or in the words of philosophy, the phylogeny (origin of a tribe, kind, or species) of the whole depends on the ontogeny (origin of being) of one. So, in evolution, for instance, some have proposed that the development of an organism (ontogeny) expresses all the intermediate forms of its ancestors throughout evolution (phylogeny). More simply, a single seed interacting with a particular context can result in a vast forest.

Contextualization yokes the permanence of a unique identity as a disciple of Jesus to the flux of cultural contexts, constructs, and conditions. To contextualize the gospel is to bring the content of the gospel and the character of Christ into conversation with the homegrown cultures of humankind in the past, present, and future.

In the real estate business, location is king: "Location, location, location." In the discipleship business, Jesus is king, but context is queen. The first rule of content is "Context, context, context." First came the content ("in the beginning was the Word"); next came the context ("and the Word was made flesh and dwelt among us"). All content has a context. There is no content without context. Even One God has a Trinitarian context.

All that I have done in my life I have done for Love, and this Love is not an abstract reality but a Person, Jesus Christ, to whom I vowed my life on my Profession day.

—Sister Mary David, OSB[40]

One of the things that most distinguishes Christianity from other religions is that it is not in the culture-making business. Christianity knows no "Christian culture." Christianity knows no "Christian cooking"; no Christian garb or fashion; no Christian banking or economics;[41] no Christian medicine; no Christian morality; no Christian language. Christianity knows nothing that separates the faithful *from* the rest of humanity or creation. Christianity is a faith only *for* the rest of humanity and creation. Whenever the word *Christian* appears as an adjective, something is wrong. And any culture that claims to be a "Christian culture" is a cult.

God made the world "good," and everything in it. We exist in relationship with the world "God so loved," not separate from it. The gospel is made incarnate in all the diverse cultures of the world. The gospel is not intended to turn all the cultures of the world into Christian cultures. In fact, the gospel promises to become something new and fresh when it is incarnated in another culture. Evangelism is not going to Afghanistan or Brazil or Cambodia or the Dominican Republic and saying, "I'm here to remake your culture." Evangelism is going to Ethiopia, Fiji, Greece, and Haiti and saying, "I'm here to incarnate Jesus in your midst so that the greater fullness of Christ can be seen in all its richness and beauty to bless the world." The former is the straitjacket of colonialism. The latter is Joseph's coat of incarnation, wide enough to jacket the world.

Culture can become a cult, and Western culture has too often become a cult. Yet the notion that just because an idea originated in Western culture it has no universal validity is as dangerous as the notion that Western culture itself is universally valid. The medieval monks who are credited with saving Western civilization did not try to save "Western culture" or "Christian civilization." They dedicated their lives to saving human culture in all its manifestations and proved it by the fact that much of what they saved was pagan writings and even erotic and atheist writings they themselves would have nothing to do with and would not have accessioned into their library under normal conditions. Monasteries were Noah's arks of safety for all humanity, not just Christianity.

Culture cults are some of the most insidious cults of all, since they're hidden right before our eyes, just as the word *cult* is hidden in the word *culture*. Whether it's Western culture or consumer culture or celebrity culture, ego culture (culture of the self) or techno-culture (technology will save us), politics culture (politics will save us) or US culture, a culture cult is idolatry and, yes, even sometimes a suicide cult. Culture cults can exist alongside each other and feed each other's worship. When idols start to synergize and dance with each other in a circle dance, they can lock the whole culture itself in a death spiral, a dance of death.

The fundamental Christian belief is that God remakes human beings from the inside out by sacrificial love, not that God remakes humanity from the outside in by cultural change. It is an old Christian metaphor of how you repair a damaged musical instrument: an amateur tries to restore it with glue, but a master craftsman works with the grain of the wood.[42] In an incarnational model, you love your way into the new; you don't work your way out of the old. You rise to the future more by exercising the promises of the past than by apprising and appraising the guises and disguises of the past.

Every context has a language, and every culture is a language. Learning to read those languages is what is called *semiotics*. Contextual intelligence is another way of talking about what every missionary does before they leave home for the mission field: learn the native vernacular and culture. "Contextualization is both inevitable and essential," contends Jackson Wu in the best book on the subject.[43] All ministry is contextual because all ministry is cross-cultural cross-bearing. You cannot escape time and place. Those who try to live outside of time open themselves up to the severe dangers of legalism, syncretism, moralism, or even a bellicose biblicism.

Christian life fails to convince because it lacks incarnate credibility.

—*Cistercian Abbot Erik Varden*[44]

Paul's understanding of contextualization was all-encompassing: "all things to all people" (1 Cor. 9:22). Every calling comes stamped and dated, bound to a particular era in time and spot in space. No ministry should be "out of date" or dateless. We seldom sing anymore the Appalachian baptismal hymn "On Jordan's Stormy Banks" that includes the repetitive refrain "I am bound for the Promised Land."[45] But one cannot be eternity bound without being time-bound.[46] We are rooted in our time even while we're routed toward eternity.

You don't get to choose your context. Appropriating Heidegger's philosophical notion of "thrownness," we are all "thrown" or "thrust" into the world in a context we did not choose. Life is not totally under our control. We get to choose the containers we use for the content, like our clothing or our coffee cups, but not the context of the content. Our context is part of an arranged marriage. In the sovereignty and providence of God, we have been wedded to a context not of our choosing but of God's. God chose our love—our context for ministry and mission. Now we must learn to love God's choice for us, the context in which God has placed us.

Moses's call to ministry included a place of service: "You shall worship God upon this mountain" (Ex. 3:12). Early bishops were known by their context (Augustine of Hippo, Lucius of Cyrene, Gaius of Ephesus), and saints by their context (Paul of Tarsus, Cyril of Jerusalem, Polycarp of Smyrna).

Jesus lived his context and loved his context—enough to cry over it. The Jesus triangulation of "in/not-of/not-out-of" culture[47] is not a one-time-for-all-time negotiation. It is a daily dance of getting in touch with your cultural partner but staying in tune with the Christ who transcends each culture but transfigures persons and communities in every culture and transplants in any culture the new reality of God's dream for a new earth and a new heaven. There is a built-in ironic distance in the biblical view of Christ and culture: You can be indigenous and diasporic at the same time.

The world is not a conclusion.

—*Emily Dickinson (1830–1886)*[48]

Why are whales so vulnerable, so fragile, yet so free and strong? Whales are mammals who live in one world but breathe the air of another.[49] Disciples of Jesus are whales. We live in the world of the here-and-now, but we breathe the air of another. We sing whale songs, the songs of the water, but we hear the music of another world that directs our song. We all pay rent in the real world, where we find our bliss, but we long for those breaths of heaven, breathings of the Spirit that remind us of the higher bliss that "surpasses all understanding" (Phil. 4:7). We are simultaneously insiders and outsiders, natives and outlanders, homesteaders and homebodies.

We are "in" this world, not "of" this world. We are in the body physically, but our spirit is with Christ, where we live in the land of Beulah. In *Pilgrim's Progress* (1678), the land of Beulah was within full view of the gates of the Celestial City. You could hear continually the singing of birds, the whistling of the woods, the flowing of water, and the singing of fountains; you could see trees hanging with fruits and plants lush with flowers. This is the Promised Land, which beckons each and every one of us. St. Paul called this land of Beulah "the heavenlies," but it was not heaven, since he also spoke of the wrestling with principalities and powers that takes place in these "heavenly places."[50]

A water boatman is a pond bug about one inch in length with long hind legs that make it a good swimmer. It lives cocooned in a silvery bubble of surface air, which it inflates above the water, and then it sinks to the bottom by attaching itself to a plant stem or stick, which sinks and anchors the floating house of air near where it can suck the bottom ooze for food. In that bubble of air, it breathes and builds its nest and breeds its young while all sorts of creatures and predators come and go, circling the dark waters and slimy depths.

We are not afraid of the predatory deep or menacing slime because we are cocooned in Christ, awaiting that day when we will shed this silken shroud and become a new creation in Christ, when "the old [caterpillar] will pass away, and all things become [butterfly] new." As the King James most properly translates Philippians 3:20, "For our conversation is in heaven; from whence also we look for the Saviour, the Lord Jesus Christ." Wherever Jesus is, there is heaven. When Christians die, they change their context, not their conversation.

Incarnation is God's creation unfolding and ongoing into human form, the unceasing rendering of spirit into flesh and its translation back into spirit again.

Contextual intelligence is based on the mystery of incarnation. Incarnation is part of one divine act: Creation. Incarnation is God's creation unfolding and ongoing into human form, the unceasing rendering of spirit into flesh and its translation back into spirit again.

There is not just one Big Bang of Incarnation, but many big bangs of incarnation. There is not just one Incarnation but ongoing incarnations. We are not making an argument here for evolution, but rather pointing to the ongoing creativity of God.

The ongoing incarnation is Jesus wanting to take up residence inside you and become part of who you are, as well as reside within your community.

When it comes to ongoing incarnation, replication is never duplication but always personalized personation. It is not the church's mission to encase people in some new suit of language. A fresh expression of the gospel will be a new incarnation that is a true inculturation, not a mechanical imposition of black-and-white sheet music on the present, but one where the *cantus firmus* (Latin: in music, a "fixed song" is a pre-existing melody forming the basis for multiple compositional possibilities) is imbued with local phrasings, improvised shadings, and soundings from the surroundings.

Contextualization is the primary and secondary scandal of the Christian story. The primary scandal? That "God so loved the world" that God would subject divine omnipotence to human incompetence, ignorance, and resistance and entrust God's precious Son to the verdicts and whims of human hands and human contexts.

The secondary scandal? "And God said, Let us make the human in our image, after our likeness" (Gen. 1:26). God made humans in the divine likeness. But to keep humans in the divine likeness, God sent God to be "made in the likeness of the human" (Phil. 2:7). In order for humans to keep being made in divine likeness, the divine had to be made in the human likeness. *Imago Dei* became *imago hominem*. The Story became a person who lived God's story among a particular people and cultural context. We beheld the beauty of his story as he walked with us in that context, full of goodness and truth.

We believe the cultivation of contextual intelligence must flow from a healthy love of the people and place where we find ourselves. God "so loved the world he gave" is not only about loving people but loving a place. New creation, or "heaven," is not about abandoning the physical cosmos but renewing it. Resurrection is not a dumpster but a recycling bin.

If we want to increase our CQ, we must start with the gesso of a healthy love of the people and place where we are. Do you love your place enough to follow the pattern of Jesus and empty yourself, taking on a posture of vulnerability? Do you weep for your zip code? Do you love your people enough to pray for them while they hang you on the cross?

Before we can join Jesus in painting the canvas of our community with a new future, we must be willing to be contextualized ourselves. We must put on flesh in the particularity of our place and release ourselves into the mystery of incarnation. We must explore how Jesus is being made incarnate afresh not only in us but in our context. If we skip this pre-work, we can be sure there will be problems with our canvas later.

CHAPTER 8

THE CQ MANDORLA RING

As physical beings, we are literally open to the world, suffused every second with air from somewhere else; as social beings, we are equally determined by our contexts.

—Jenny Odell[51]

A mandorla is an almond-shaped area of light, widely used in Christian iconograpy to surround sacred individuals. The pointed oval figure, also used as an architectural feature, can be created by the overlapping of two circles.

The *CQ Mandorla* outlines a very simple process of contextualization that can be summarized in the symbol of two overlapping circles that birth a third almond-shaped ring (mandorla) and four words that formularize the process: BE THERE WITH ALL. The sweet spot of contextual ministry is found in that mandorla overlapping space of Connectedness that metabolizes the first circle of Content (BE) with the second circle of Context (THERE), creating the third space of Connectedness (WITH). Hence BE (Content) THERE (Context) WITH (Connection) All (Cosmos).

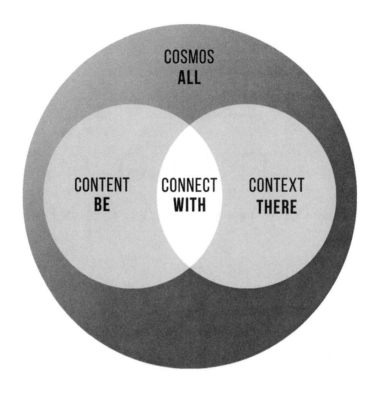

Figure 2: The CQ Mandorla Ring

Be: Content is fixed.

There: Context is flux.

With: Connection is flow.

All: Cosmos is fulfillment.

> *All the biblical commandments stem from a first basic and utterly simple commandment, namely "Be!" "Be what you are!"*
>
> —*French historian and Sorbonne professor Rémi Brague*[52]

Continuity is not fixity. The church has thrived throughout the ages not by staying in the same fixed structural state but by redefining and finding re-expression in the flux and flow of a multitude of fresh ways. When we decorate a house, to be contextual (flux) means you can get into rearranging the furniture all you want (flow), but leave the foundation untouched (fixed).

For example, the "know the times" mandate of CQ is to be incarnational, "in" but not "of" this ego culture and its orgies of self-righteousness. Jesus teaches his followers that the life of self-transcendence and the way to find oneself is by losing oneself. For Christians to seek meaning and "mindfulness" in this selfie context by the cultivation of interiority, self-centeredness, and self-discovery is to be so far "in" the world we have become "of" the world. This fails to meet the requirement of the second half of Issachar's secret to "know what to do."

If you properly connect all the dots of your context using the tried-and-true thread of content, you come up with picture of Jesus and what he is up to in that place and space. Jesus is the world's most rewritten character: Superman, Spiderman, Batman, and Wonder Woman are just a few of the messiah figures that tap in to the Jesus story. Hollywood at times has shown more interest in being "true" to the True North character and content of Jesus than portrayals in corporate culture ("Jesus CEO") and celebrity culture ("Jesus as Leader"), whose primary allegiance has been to the flux and fluidity of the cultural moment.

> *Lois, you say the world doesn't need a savior, but every day I hear people crying for one.*
>
> —*Superman Returns*

Contextual intelligence involves living the fixed Jesus story (content) through the flux of indigenous cultural elements (context) and expressing that contextualized flow (connection) in order that the fullness of Christ and the faithfulness of the church be embodied with such local integrity that there is universal resonance (cosmos).[53] In Roman Catholic terms, this is the process of *inculturation*, which integrates the life of faith (content) within the local traditions and customs of a people and place (context). The inculturation of the gospel becomes an animating force giving that culture a new orientation and recreating it (connection). Thus, within that culture a new "communion" emerges, which in its turn enriches the church universal and creation itself (cosmos).

John Wesley is famous for saying, "The world is my parish." But the world is our parish *only after we make our parish our world.* The way to the global is through the local. Love your postal code and know its strengths and weaknesses. When a church is like a Christmas round-robin letter, addressed to no one in particular, it becomes a bubble of self-focused babble and not enough of an encircling embrace.

CONTENT—be: Content is Jesus, the Christ who is fixed—"the same yesterday, today, and forever." A God who is unchanging, a God you can count on to stay true to the covenant. A God before whom you don't have to cower each morning, wondering, "What kind of mood are you in today?" This was a radical concept in the ancient world.

Tradition is good. When someone boasts, "I'm not traditional," we want to respond: "OK, so what does that make you? Transient? Temporary? Feckless? Interim?" Tradition means you give voice and vote to the past as well as to the future. Tradition means you daily "break bread with the dead," as the poet W. H. Auden put it somewhere. You sit at the feet of the ancestors, listen to their wisdom, and live out of the double meaning of the acronym "RIP." You want your ancestors to "Rest in Peace." But you also want them to "Rest in Power." When tradition is an activity, more a verb than a noun, life becomes a double spiral, the conversations between the living and the dead, the past and the future, always swirling, always ongoing, in either direction, whirling around the real swoosh, the swoosh of the Spirit, whose nucleus is Christ.

A trip down memory lane can be a bad trip or a good trip. A bad trip if you live there. A good trip if memory lane drives you farther down highways of understanding and powers greater insights into the present and incites deeper hungers for a foretaste of the future and a foretoken of "thy kingdom come." We hamstring the Holy Spirit when we only look for and listen to its stirrings in old systems and structures. Often the Spirit speaks through new voices, visions, and ventures.

Man does not have a stable existence at all, but he hurries in a perpetual vanishing, precisely like music.

—*Soren Kierkegaard*[54]

The earliest Gospel is Mark, written by one of Peter's disciples, John Mark (or some even suspect it was Peter's memoir, handed over to John Mark). Mark starts with an ambiguous genitive—"the gospel of Jesus Christ" (1:1)—which makes it equally possible to translate this as "This is the beginning of the gospel about Jesus Christ" or "This is the beginning of the gospel which is Jesus Christ."

There are liberals, there are conservatives, there are progressives, there are moderates, and then there are followers of Jesus. We believe it is time for all parties—liberal, conservative, progressive, regressive—to lay aside their weapons of mass deconstruction and disinformation and feast their eyes upon Jesus, the author and finisher of our story.

Everyone else shouts good news from every mountain top. Christians seem to like to keep good news to themselves. What is the good news? It is one word: Jesus. Jesus is the gospel. As Mark 1:1 reminds us, the "good news" is Jesus himself. Jesus is the content of Christianity. There is nothing more contemporary than the cross. There is nothing more relevant than the resurrection. There is nothing more present-day than Pentecost. There is no more current story than our parent story of Adam, Eve, and the Garden.

When you get Jesus, you also get the Scripture and the Spirit. The three together form the Holy Braid. There are three threads God designed to be plaited, or woven, into one braid of revelation, one embroidery of truth. The Bible is the inspired, authoritative, God-breathed Story of God. The subject of the Scripture is the Jesus Story, the only story you can trust your life to. When the three strands of Story, Spirit, and Savior are tightly twined, there is nothing stronger: "a threefold cord is not easily broken" (Eccl. 4:12). They are untwined at the Humpty-Dumpty peril of "all fall down." They are embellished or accessorized at the peril of falsification, which is the alternative meaning of *embroider*. The relationship between hearing Jesus through the Scripture and under the inspiration of the Holy Spirit is the centerpiece content of biblical theology.

Reading Scripture is the key to reading life, both of which stand at the heart of following Jesus.

The Bible bears gifts richer and more valuable than those brought to a child by wise ones two thousand years ago. Reading Scripture is the key to reading life, both of which stand at the heart of following Jesus. Do not let this gift pass by unopened. "Take the Bible in one hand and the daily newspaper in the other" is how Karl Barth is usually quoted. But the actual quote is a little more nuanced: "Take your Bible and take your newspaper and read both. But interpret newspapers from your Bible."[55]

It's no longer the "daily newspaper" but TGIF media (Twitter, Google,

Instagram, Facebook) and the local neighborhood news. The point is that you cannot separate content and context, the content of Scripture and the context of a specific culture.

> *Down the long lane of history yet to be written, America knows that this world of ours, growing ever smaller, must avoid becoming a community of dreadful fear and hate, and must, instead, be a proud confederation of mutual trust and respect.*
>
> —*President Dwight D. Eisenhower (1890–1969)*[56]

CONTEXT—there: One of us used a refrain periodically to call people to worship. It was a new ministry plant, and the congregation loved to give this unison response to this opening question:

"Why are we all here?"

"Because we're not all there."

To be "there" in a state of all-ness and all-there-ness is one of the greatest moments of anyone's life.

For an anthropologist, the saying goes, "Context is everything." In reading the Bible, or in reading another person, context is key. In the old saying that every preacher wants to claim, for themselves or from an ancestor, "A text without a context is a pretext for a proof text." For a Christian, however, content is everything. Context is next to everything. The Word (content) became flesh (context). Context is the essence of incarnation. As we've said before, content is king. Context is queen.

Context is more than a matter of remembering when you go to England that elevators are lifts, gas is petrol, and there are no zucchini, eggplant, or arugula over there, only courgettes, aubergines, and rocket. The context will help determine the containers in which the content is delivered and connections are made and from which the character of Christ is formed.

Again, consider how Jesus taught the disciples to learn from, and situate themselves in, their surroundings—to look, observe, consider, behold, watch:

> *"Look at the birds of the air; they neither sow nor reap nor gather into barns, and yet your heavenly Father feeds them. Are you not of more value than they? And can any of you by worrying add a single hour to your span of life? And why do you worry about clothing? Consider the lilies of the field, how they grow; they neither toil nor spin, yet I tell you, even Solomon in all his glory was not clothed like one of these."*
>
> —*Matthew 6:26–29*

Jesus was teaching his disciples the value of placefulness. Know your "there" (place), love your place, and see how God is at work in your place. Also see what's fragmented about your place. Jesus exhibits contextual intelligence in action by minding the gaps and disorienting the systems of his day. He showcased the difference between a natural hierarchy and a power hierarchy. Power hierarchy is enforced from the top down, and you get "fit in" like a piece of a puzzle. Natural hierarchy emerges from the bottom up, and you get to "fit together" organically, based on your Spirit-given gifts planted throughout the body to live and serve God in the world.

Jesus wasn't always nice. He could be quite adept at healthy conflict. The greatest prophetic voice ever heard confronted the dominant mental models and power hierarchies by reframing the sacred texts and traditions ("you've heard it said, but I say"). In fact, Jesus claimed to be a Torah guy himself. He believed Torah was true. He also announced that he came to embody Torah. He himself was Torah True, and his mission as Embodied Torah was to "fulfill" Torah (Matt. 5:17). Yet his fulfillment could be a radical reframing of Torah as it was interpreted in his day. His drumbeat of disputes with the Pharisees made this loud and clear (Deut. 24:1; Mark 10:2–9). For example, Jesus transfigures "eye for an eye" into "turn the other cheek," and "hate your enemies" becomes "love your enemies and pray for them" (Matt 5:17–48).

Jesus contextualizes Scripture not only by embodying Scripture as "living word" (John 1:1); he also directly reframes incarnationally whole sections of the Torah—for example, in the Book of Leviticus, where it speaks of "clean versus unclean" sins requiring the death penalty and the crass restrictions of those with birth defects, the deformed, or menstruating women not being allowed in community worship.[57] Jesus's radical missional reading of Scripture, his "Temple tantrum,"[58] and an unpopular position on the inevitable destruction of the Temple were profound disruptions to the religious system. To the religious establishment of his day, Jesus was not a positive deviant but rather a provocateur at best, a betrayer at worst.

> *The perception that God is in this situation and we are called to find him here and now is a very great gift of grace.*
>
> *—Sister Mary David Totah, OSB (1957–2017), Prioress of St Cecilia's Abbey*[59]

John Wesley Powell is a case study in CQ. He paid attention to his place. In a sense, he prophesied the coming Dust Bowl, but no one listened to him, and worse, they laughed at him. He read his "there," in this case the geography of the United States, and in 1877 drew a longitudinal line from Mexico to Canada (100th Meridian) that separated the United States into an arid West and a verdant East, and showed how silly the 1862 Homestead Act was for those given their 160 acres west of the 100th Meridian. He was finally vindicated when a ten-thousand-foot-tall dust cloud— the Black Duster— descended on Washington, DC. Western senators got him fired from his longtime directorship of the United States Geological Survey Office.

Powell knew his "there" intimately. He calculated that you need twenty inches of rain a year to grow crops. Aridity of the West means that without irrigation, no matter how many acres you get, it's a black future of bankruptcy, and Powell was a Manifest Destiny guy. He believed in westward expansion and nation-building. He believed in human engineering and the power of man over nature. He was tainted by his time. But he also believed that you needed to expand with intelligence and with sensitivity to the topography, the weather, the stewardship of the land—the "there" of be, *there*, with, all.

Louie Pasteur is another case in point. His on-site laboratories at the scene of major problems, reading from within context, then through experimentation, developing solutions (knowing what to do). He saved the sheep and cattle farmers' livelihood, figured out how to prevent wine from spoiling, and saved the silk industry. While everyone else was back in the lab, trying to figure it out from an ivory tower, he was in the trenches of the problem, reading the signs. That is more about CQ than IQ.

For a more recent example, think of Bill Gates's now famous 2015 TED talk, where he accurately predicted a coming pandemic crisis.[60] In 2018, Gates again noted the coming of a disease that within six months could potentially kill 30 million people.[61] An Issacharian, he was reading the signs of the times and proposing what to do, highlighting the lack of pandemic preparedness. Unfortunately, as in so many cases with contextually intelligent persons, nobody listened.

Rev. Will Conner pastors a small rural congregation in Decatur, Tennessee. He was able to read the signs of his community and guide his congregation regarding what to do. He noticed the growing poverty in his area and how people would come to receive food and clothing from his church but were not connected to the worshiping congregation. Rather than trying to funnel people back to the Sunday morning services, he planted a contextual form of church with children and young families involving fun, crafts, and a meal. Over time, by responding to the context, this new Christian community, a "Messy Church" along with the inherited congregation, is growing.

Rev. Conner was "minding the gaps," seeing the sore spots, the fragmentation, the disconnects in his community, the institutional voids where his church could build relational bridges. Pioneers like Will see the gaps as opportunities for social innovation. They are able to bridge those gaps and create new things between what is and what could be. In this case, he leveraged the relational capital his church already enjoyed to create a new form of Christian community. We will explore these concepts through the Contextual Intelligence Framework more fully later.

Jesus commissioned us to incarnate the gospel in all native cultures, in every context, not to spend all our firepower condemning the native culture. Wait—even if that culture is a celebrity, consumer, or anti-Christian culture? Yes. When the widow gave her all in her offering at the Temple, Jesus commended her actions, even though Jesus knew full well how corrupt the Temple had become and that he was going to suffer at the hands of those in power at the Temple. If "God so loved the world" with all of its evil and sin and shame, what's our problem?

> *The Story became a Song, an artist who sang God's story among us, and we reveled in his beauty as he walked with us, trailing goodness and truth.*
>
> —*John 1:14 (our translation)*

Contextual intelligence requires us to get comfortable with paradox, to escape either/or thinking and move to and/also thinking. Something can be true in one context and not in another. For example, a Methodist or Baptist pastor may be required to do four or five services in one day but canon law decrees a priest can't say more than three masses on a Sunday.

Disciples are incarnators, but the incarnation, the Incarnate One, Jesus the Christ, cuts both ways: to communicate and to conceal, to speak and to withdraw, toward greater clarity and toward greater mystery. Part of revelation, apocalypse, leans toward greater unveiling and clarity; but part of revelation, apocalypse, is toward incomprehension, paradox, and mystery. To live as incarnators is to live the meaning and the mystery at the same time, to embrace what Shakespeare, at the close of *King Lear*, called "the mystery of things."

> *"He is destined to be a sign which men reject; many in Israel will stand or fall because of him."*
>
> —*Luke 2:34*

Ann E. Nelson (1958–2019) was one of the most prestigious and pioneering particle physicists in the world. From her chair at the University of Washington, she conducted research and wrote papers that dominated the top ten cited scholars in her field. After Dr. Nelson's tragic death from a hiking fall in the Alpine Lakes Wilderness in Washington State, a former student and then colleague in cosmology at the University of New Hampshire, Chanda Prescod-Weinstein, wrote in a *Quanta* magazine tribute, "Ann told me that to be happy as a model builder in particle physics, I had to be O.K. with something like mounting a moose head on a wall and putting a purple scarf on it and not worrying about why it was wearing a purple scarf." Given how strange supersymmetry and particle physics really is, the metaphor would have been better with a mounted mouse head scarfed in purple than a moose head. But it is more than ironic that our best scientists are more open to living with mystery and serendipity, the unknown and the unfamiliar, than many theologians and Christians.[62]

CONNECT—with: Once the content overlaps with the context, the fixed and the flux meld and merge, recode[63] and reframe,[64] there is triggered a flow of connection that turns on the operating system (OS) for Christianity: MRI (Missional, Relational, Incarnational).[65] There will be many interfaces that will work, depending on the changing historical and cultural context. The EPIC (Experiential, Participatory, Image-Rich, Connectional) interface seems to work best in a TGIF (Twitter, Google, Instagram, Facebook) context. But interfaces come and go. The operating system remains the same. Or should. The mark of true connection is when the flow is Missional, Relational, Incarnational (MRI). All contextuality needs a missionary consciousness. All contextuality needs a relational matrix. All contextuality needs an incarnational reading of the culture.

The church is no stranger to the liminality of the "with." There are multiple occasions provided in Scripture of God's people moving through the process of in-betweenness and withness. The movement from favor to unfavor with Pharaoh (Ex. 1:8), the forty-year wandering in the wilderness between liberation from captivity and Promised Land (Josh. 5:6), the emergence of the judges and a new generation who "did not know" YHWH (Judg. 2), the rocky transition of kingship between Saul and David (1 Chron. 11–12), the captivity and exile with an accompanying Jeremiahian logic to settle in for the long haul (Jer. 29), Jesus in the tomb (Mark 15:46), the church prayerfully awaiting the Spirit (Acts 2), and many more.

One of the most influential theologians of the twentieth century, Paul Tillich, made it a philosophical mandate and maxim never to separate the particular and the universal. He made this hermeneutical axiom into an axis for everything he wrote: "Particularize in order to universalize." Although Tillich did not mention where he got his axiom, you can find this dance of ontogeny and phylogeny, the global and the local, the cosmic and the parochial in the very beginning of the Bible, where we find both a macro and a micro creation narratives.

All people should be loved equally. But you cannot do good to all people equally, so you should take particular thought for those who, as if by lot, happen to be particularly close to you in terms of place, time, or any other circumstances.

—*St. Augustine*[66]

Every person deserves the right to be seen in their particularity, not as a personality type or psychological syndrome or in terms of their professional résumé or generational grouping or economic status.[67] Only in the light of full particularity does a subject take on universal, theological significance. In fact, an early usage of the word *occasional* (just as Goethe, for example, used the word) meant responding to a particular moment or occasion with integrity and authenticity without being flippant, casual, or generic.

"Just a Closer Walk" with Jesus doesn't take place in a vacuum. You sometimes take a closer walk with Jesus in the sunshine of sycamores. At other times you take a closer walk with Jesus in the vale of cypress and the valley of yew, the garden of olives or the sepulcher of stones.

We are made into nations and tribes that we may know and love each other.

—*Koran*

Who is my neighbor? Anyone anywhere any time in need is my neighbor. Neighborliness starts at home but doesn't end there. Doing what is before us causes us to do what is beyond us. One of us has flown more than six million miles in their lifetime. You might say one of us has been almost everywhere but seen very little anywhere. The way to the universal is through the particular.[68]

What can prevent us from finding Jesus's sandals in the dust of our zip code? What hobbles us from connecting the content and the context and ministering in the overlap of the with?

Our epistemic vices (*epistemic* relates to knowledge, and vices are the opposite of virtues, meaning the reduced ways of thinking we often employ) are primary hindrances, of course. These epistemic vices feature arrogance, closed-mindedness, gullibility.[69] These obstruct our reading of the signs because they make us less sensitive to the evidence for and against our own views and preferences. We ignore, misuse, and overlook evidence or even fail to look where we think we might find it in the first place.

Another reason why it is so hard to see God at work and at play in our world today? Jesus gave us a reason: "Blessed are the pure in heart, for they shall see God" (Matt. 5:8). Purity of heart gives us the second sight of trust, ESP for the divine. Trust is the spyglass to trace the Spirit. Control is the blinder that blocks the Son. Everything builds on trust. When trust goes, everything goes, gives way, and collapses. Rebuilding is futile until trust is rebuilt.

Sell your cleverness, and buy bewilderment.

—*Rumi*

A third reason is our diminished capacity for wonder and even for worship. Our walk must be unhurried, our pauses and stops aplenty. The first European to travel the length of the Amazon was Francisco Orellana (1511–1546). In fact, the Amazon River was initially named Rio de Orellana to honor his journey. Orellana was dispatched by Gonzalo Pizarro in 1541 to find some food to support his mission to find the land of El Dorado.

Orellana sailed down the Rio Nap, a swift river in eastern Ecuador. When he finally reached the confluence of the Ucayali River, as the Upper Amazon is known in Peru, he went temporarily insane. He only knew the parched landscape of Spain and could not imagine a river on God's earth that could possibly be so enormous. Little did he know what awaited him two thousand miles downstream, where the Amazon becomes a sea and the riverbanks lie a hundred miles apart.[70] Many of us live in such little boxes of mind and spirit that we can't fathom the signs of the God of the universe loving our little town or village or city enough to die for it.

COSMOS—all: God gives "to all men all life, and breath, and all things" (Acts 17:24–25). But an *all* without a *with* amounts to nothing in particular. The singularity of all depends on the individuality of each. Only withness leads to all-there-ness.

> *Variety's the very spice of life*
> *That gives it all its flavor.*
> *—William Cowper (1731–1800), "The Task"*

Arguably the simplest yet densest, the most elementary but elemental six words in our sacred story are these: "Christ is all and in all" (Col. 3:11). Aside from *Christ*, none of the words when written in English is more than three letters, and all are monosyllables.

Yet this *all* revelation is the neutron star of all revolution. When the crust of those six simple words is burst open, there is a juddering, jolting, vibrating explosion of energy called a Starquake.[71] After a Starquake, "all things are made new" (2 Cor. 5:17). Jesus is the Starquake of the universe.

The love of Christ will not let us go, but it will not let us off either. It will not let us off the hook or let us get away with not doing what we know we should do. The Starquake of the universe draws all to itself.

Why is it that nobody understands me and everybody likes me?

—Albert Einstein (1879–1955)[72]

God so loved the cosmos, the *all*, that God deigned to stoop to the particular and initiated our connection *with* the One. *With* is the heart of Emmanuel ("God with us"). The life of Jesus, his witness and withness, is the ultimate form of contextual intelligence. God transfigures creation by entering fully into it, taking on the particularity of *with* to redeem *all*. God takes on a particular withness, a fully human, fully sensory experience, to reach allness. The content of the universe enters into the context of a human life. God transfigures creation by entering fully into it and being with it, taking on particularity to redeem universally.

God takes on a fully human, fully sensory experience. Jesus *of* Nazareth fully immerses himself in the language, culture, and practices of a seemingly insignificant place. It is the resonance of an authentic contextual voice, the voice of a specific place and time, that speaks universally to all humanity. You cannot be there for *all* until you are *with* one. God doesn't merely love in general but in the particular. Jesus didn't just love people, he loved particular persons. We love not in universals but in particulars. To departicularize is to dehumanize. To clump and lump and label is to libel.

> *Jesus didn't just love people, he loved particular persons. We love not in universals but in particulars.*

Can the church do some unlearning, awaken from its apostolic amnesia, pay attention to the point of all-there-ness, and attune itself to the activities of the Holy Spirit in its various contexts? Perhaps the greater challenge is to "know what to do." If we take our cues from Jesus and the early church, some adaptation is before us.

We hope the CQ Mandorla Ring is a tool your team can use to find the sweet spot of contextual ministry. Here are some simple questions you can use to apply it:

1. BE (content): Where are you discovering Jesus at work in your community? How are you making people aware of Jesus in their midst when they may not be aware?

2. THERE (context): What do you know about your place? In what ways are you intentionally learning more about your context?

3. WITH (connect): How are you being with the people in your community? Not doing ministry *to* them or *for* them, but finding ways to be *with* them?

4. ALL (cosmos): Who is missing from your ministry that lives in your zip code? Who are you directly or indirectly withdrawing your withness from? How can you change this?

Jesus and his disciples read the signs, immersed themselves relationally in the context of people's daily lives, and became a community of transfiguration within it, which had salvific power for all without it. The one intelligence to serve all multiple intelligences is contextual intelligence. Let us show you what we mean.

CHAPTER 9

THE ONE RING

One Intelligence to Serve Them All

The key to leading effectively is knowing the things that make up your environment and then helping to arrange them so that their power becomes available.

—Sun Tzu, *The Art of War*

In this chapter we want to explore how contextual intelligence relates to and amplifies all the other intelligences. Understanding this interaction is important for leaders who want to help their churches grow a high CQ. Cultivating CQ leads to healthier missional, relational, and incarnational engagement as we seek to know, love, and serve our communities.

In J. R. R. Tolkien's *Lord of the Rings* series, the One Ring was an artifact of incredible power. Crafted by the Dark Lord Sauron in the fires of Mount Doom, the single ring could exercise control over the other rings of power, therefore bringing all peoples under Sauron's tyrannical rule. Rather than serving a dark lord who seeks to rule over all others, those under the lordship of Jesus are to become servants of others, bringing reconciliation and healing where there is fragmentation. In the CQ Mandorla Ring, contextual intelligence is the *all* that brings together and unites the other multiple intelligences. It is the one intelligence to serve them all.

Take IQ, for example. The validity and reliability of IQ tests have been challenged for decades. By now it is apparent that standardized tests measure one specific form of intelligence—the ability to take tests, or, more precisely, Enlightenment-based tests. Furthermore, the idea that high IQ predicts career success is fanciful.

We do not deny that IQ (intelligence quotient) and EQ (emotional quotient) are surely important. But we believe that what we are calling CQ (contextual intelligence quotient) is what is most needed in the church today. In fact, only CQ has the potential to bring all the other component intelligences together into one whole intelligence. Again, contextual intelligence is literally about accurately reading between the lines. The CQ skill is the ability to accurately diagnose a context and make correct decisions regarding what to do to meet and greet the future.

Admittedly, there is no conclusive agreement about what the concept of intelligence really is. Some concepts of intelligence orient on achievement, others on aptitude. Traditionally, a *general intelligence* or *g*, has been considered a universal trait possessed by individuals at various levels. In the West, we largely associate this general intelligence with linguistic and logical-mathematical abilities. We measure this capacity with the IQ produced by standardized tests.[73] Those individuals with genius IQs are deemed exceptional among the human species. In short, intelligence has been researched in the past primarily in relation to the internal world of the individual.

Increasingly, this psychometric paradigm has been challenged within the field of psychology, especially cross-cultural psychology.[74] Most already concede that standardized IQ testing has a cultural bias and does not seriously consider external forces. While IQ tests have been continuously refined to be as "culture fair" as possible, it is highly questionable if these tests are able to escape measuring a specific form of Western academic or analytical intelligence. Is IQ testing merely a tool to measure the ability to take tests? Some psychologists insist that the general intelligence factor that IQ tests measure predicts school grades and job performance equally well. Other studies demonstrate a lack of strong correlation between actual occupational performance and IQ scores.

A quick glance at most career fields demonstrates the lack of correlation between school grades and occupational success. In fact, it appears as if the world is run by C+ students. Long before David Halberstam traced the origins of our worst and stupidest war to *The Best and the Brightest* (1972), research revealed that those IQ tests measured as the "brightest" were seldom the "best."[75]

The idea of multiple intelligences can be traced as far back as Aristotle's triarchic theory of intelligence as theoretical, practical, and productive. Steinberg's analytical, practical, and creative intelligences, which will inform our exploration of contextual intelligence, closely resemble—although are not drawn from—Aristotle's triarchic model.[76] But while theories of multiple intelligences are not new, they have gained considerable traction both among theorists[77] and the general population in the last several decades.[78] The many proponents of these theories base their claims on valid research, have produced a tidal wave of popular books, and have transformed educational environments and work place systems alike.

The biggest learning tsunamis were released by two distinguished psychologists in the early 1980s: Howard Gardner's *Theory of Multiple Intelligences* and Robert Sternberg's ground-breaking *Triarchic Theory of Intelligence*. In 1983, Howard Gardner published *Frames of Mind: The Theory of Multiple Intelligences*. Following in the footsteps of psychologists like L. L. Thurstone (1960) and J. P. Guilford (1967), he argued against the widely accepted premise that all human beings possesses a single intelligence, which psychologists call *g* for *general intelligence*.

Rather than one *g*, Gardner claimed humans possess "a set of relatively autonomous intelligences" that provide distinct sets of processing operations that permit a wide range of activities that are contextually appropriate. While some psychologists have dismissed Gardner's theory as pseudo-psychology that lacks a significant grounding in empirical research, his theory has unquestionably and profoundly impacted educational and workplace systems. Gardner proposes three distinct uses of the term *intelligence*:[79]

1. A property of all human beings. All possess multiple intelligences.

2. A dimension on which human beings differ. All people—even identical twins—possess different profiles of intelligences.

3. The way in which one carries out a task in virtue of one's goals.

For our purposes, the most helpful aspect of the multiple intelligences tradition is the focus on *contextualization*. The growing trend in the behavioral sciences is for scholars to take seriously crucial differences among the contexts where human beings live and grow. No intelligence can develop outside of interactions with the culture one inhabits. While Gardner's theory of multiple intelligences acknowledges this contextual interaction, Robert Sternberg advances it significantly in his 1984 publication, "Toward a Triarchic Theory of Human Intelligence."

Sternberg was the first to propose a contextual framework for understanding intelligence. The Triarchic Theory of Intelligence identifies three large interacting intelligences: 1. analytical intelligence, or information processing skills; 2. creative intelligence, the capacity to solve novel problems; and 3. practical intelligence, application of intellectual skills to everyday situations. The strength of this theory is how it takes into account a balance of these three intelligences interacting within a context and does not reduce intelligence to a purely individualistic inner force.

Sternberg viewed intelligence in context as consisting of intentional *adaptation to, shaping of, and selection of real-world environments relevant to one's life.* His contextual perspective provided a bold escape from the confining psychometric view that gave rise to both the IQ test and the questionable assumption that tests can accurately measure intelligence in isolation. Intelligence must be considered in light of adaptive behavior in the real-world environment.[80] The nature of intelligence is indecipherable without understanding how interaction with the environment shapes what constitutes intelligent behavior in a given sociocultural context.

According to Sternberg, we need internal analyses that can explain cognitive processes coupled with external analyses that can make clear which behaviors or classes of behavior are intelligent in varying environments. Thus, he sees these analyses as being of equal value in measuring intelligence.[81]

Sternberg shows us that *intelligent behavior* is often not intelligent universally across all cultures. Later, he further developed his theory to describe the combination of these analytical, creative, and practical dimensions as *successful intelligence.* Analytical intelligence is focused on applying strategies, acquiring task-relevant and metacognitive knowledge, and engaging in self-regulation. Creative intelligence is focused on solving novel problems and developing processing skills to become automatic, which then frees working memory for complex thinking. Practical intelligence is goal-oriented activity aimed at adapting to, shaping, or selecting environments.[82]

In other words, IQ scores do not equate with career success.[83] Adapting, shaping, and choosing environments is essential to applying analytical and creative intelligence in actual contexts. Look at the stars in any given field of endeavor and ask what distinguishes such persons from all the rest? Sternberg calls attention to two distinguishing characteristics:

1. at least one extraordinarily well-developed skill

2. an extraordinary ability to capitalize upon that skill or skills in their work

Intelligence, as it operates in the everyday world, depends on contextual interactions and demands we distinguish "book smarts" from "street smarts."

Intelligence, as it operates in the everyday world, depends on contextual interactions and demands we distinguish "book smarts" from "street smarts."

Sternberg posits that "underlying successful performance in many real-world tasks is a set of judgmental skills based upon tacit understanding of a kind that is never explicitly taught, and, in many instances, never even verbalized."[84]

Not only did Gardner's theory of multiple intelligences challenge the assumption that traditional types of intelligence, such as IQ, fail to fully explain cognitive ability. But also his introduction of the personal intelligences opened the door wide for multiple new forms of intelligence to be explored. Perhaps most importantly among these is emotional intelligence (EQ), which was first proposed by psychologists Peter Salovey and John Mayer, but was popularized into a household name by Daniel Golemans blockbuster *Emotional Intelligence: Why It Can Matter More than IQ (1995)*.[85] Emotional Intelligence is the capacity to be aware of, control, and express one's emotions, and to be empathetic with others.

Contextual intelligence must not be confused with two other kinds of

CQs, creative intelligence and cultural intelligence—two different concepts emerging from two diverse streams of inquiry but intersecting in various ways. Creative intelligence is a term used broadly and loosely because it groups together cognitive and noncognitive aspects of creative generation, like passion and motivation, with environmental variables and thinking processes. *Cultural intelligence* is the ability to interact across cultures[86] and, in the words of Thomas and Inkson, "being skilled and flexible about understanding a culture, interacting with it to learn more about it, reshaping your thinking to have more empathy for it, and becoming more skilled when interacting with others from it."[87]

> *I will teach you differences.*
>
> *—phrase from* King Lear *Ludwig Wittgenstein in considering its use as the motto for his masterpiece* Philosophical Investigations *(published posthumously 1953)*

Context is a larger concept than culture and describes the environment and ethos that form a setting from which culture may emerge. Cultures emerge as solutions to the universal problem of how to adapt to a context. Each cultural group interacts with a context: the physical environment, geography, climate, time, and economic, political, social, religious factors. Context is the cradle of culture, the larger web of interactions where cultures grow and thrive. Thus, a single context may consist of multiple cultures interacting with each other.

The contextual intelligence quotient (CQ) builds on, embraces, and enmeshes interactions with all the multiple intelligences, such as intelligence quotient (IQ), emotional quotient (EQ), cultural intelligence (CQ), creative intelligence (CQ), adversity intelligence (AQ), digital intelligence (DQ) or media intelligence (MQ), social intelligence (SQ), and personal intelligence (UQ, for self-knowledge or You Quotient). All of these various intelligences are indispensable in the cultivation of contextual intelligence—one intelligence to serve them all.[88]

In short, a context is a complex system, a system of systems within larger systems within larger systems, some of which are expanding and some of which are shrinking.[89] And the motto of all complex systems is this: "Adapt or die."

At times our ancestors in the faith invoked a caveat when they engaged in theological discussion or debate. When arriving at some consensus or conclusion about matters of the divine, they would sometimes end the discussion with the Latin phrase *"Deo semper maior,"* which in English translates to "God is always greater." Twelfth-century theologian Anselm made this phrase into a daily precept and definitional precision about God, whom he defined as "that which nothing greater can be conceived." Whatever is the greatest you can think of, Anselm said? Deo semper maior. God is always greater.

All discussion about multiple intelligences needs to end in *Deo semper maior*. Give it your best shot. Bring it on. Think as hard as you can about contextualizing the ways and whys of God. But remember, God is always greater. God is "able to do exceedingly abundantly above all that we can ask or think" (Eph. 3:20), precisely because God is always greater than we can ask or think. How would these four words—*God is always greater*—change church discussions if we used it as a PS to all our deliberations?

> *Lord, forgive us and deliver us from always thinking about ourselves and not thinking about you, your greatness, and about others and their gifts and the wonderful world you have given us that is filled with so much diversity and wonderment. Amen.*

Can CQ be measured? Can it be cultivated? Polanyi first posited the existence of tacit knowledge, an inarticulate intelligence or a kind of practical know-how that usually is not openly expressed or stated and which must be acquired in the absence of direct instruction.[90] Researchers have assessed contextual intelligence primarily as a form tacit knowledge. Wagner and Sternberg show through studies of career success in both academic and business management settings that this tacit, or practical, knowledge is one of the strongest predictors of real-world success.[91] This, however, presents a challenge regarding the measurement and cultivation of CQ.

Emerging learnings from the field of psychology and cognitive neuroscience demonstrate that CQ is something that can be practiced and even mastered. Brown, Gould, and Foster created a framework for developing contextual intelligence, noting that "intelligent performance" is the appropriate measure and suggesting three criteria: (a) one must demonstrate the ability to enact intelligent performance on authentic (real-life) tasks; (b) the ability to enact intelligent performance must persist over time; and (c) the ability must be transferable to a variety of real-life situations.[92]

We will draw from the collective intelligence of many great minds and weave these emerging learnings together in a simple framework. Yet the core of this framework is based primarily in the greatest mind in universal history . . . the mind of Christ.

PART II

KNOWING WHAT TO DO

(IMPLEMENTATION)

Of Issachar, those who had understanding of the times, to know what Israel ought to do, and all their kindred under their command.

—1 CHRONICLES 12:32

CHAPTER 10

THE CONTEXTUAL INTELLIGENCE FRAMEWORK

Your work occurs within history and in a specific place. It's important to locate yourself within the history of other struggles. How are you participating in and contributing to the human experience? It's also important to ground yourself in place, accepting responsibility for where you are, what has happened here, what can be learned from being here.

—Margaret Wheatley[93]

Now that we have described and provided a theological foundation for contextual intelligence, we can provide a framework for its cultivation. This is a brief introduction to the contextual intelligence framework (CIF). The FYSAs we explore later will be a set of competencies associated with each of the six moves: unlearning, immersion, minding the gaps, disorientation, discovery, and embodiment.

The person of Jesus, his journey of incarnation, cross, resurrection, ascension, and sending of the Spirit, is the foundation for the framework we propose. That story is our framework, and the passages we will now explore in conversation together inform that journey.

The Mind of Christ

This contextual intelligence framework, grounded in the incarnation of Jesus, is primarily sourced in the mind of Christ, the greatest manifestation of contextual intelligence in history. Jesus bequeathed his contextual intelligence to the church when he gave her this mind. We believe this is the center of the contextual intelligence framework embedded in the Scriptures, inspired by the Holy Spirit, through the reed pen of Paul.

> *Let the same mind be in you that was in Christ Jesus.*
> *—Apostle Paul*

One of the problems Paul was addressing in the early church was the phenomenon of what he described as a "blinded mind/understanding" ἐσκοτισμένοι (*skotizō*) τῇ διανοίᾳ (*dianoia*) (Eph. 4:18). Quite literally "to cover with darkness" or metaphorically "the blinding" (*skotizō*) and the "mind" (*nous*) or "mindset" (*dianoia*). The *nous* refers to the mind, the intellectual faculty, the understanding, or, more specifically, a particular mode of thinking and judging. This latter usage is more appropriately what we would understand as a mindset, a frame of mind, or an established set of attitudes—a framework through which our thinking flows.

A Blinded Mindset

> *They are darkened in their understanding, alienated from the life of God because of their ignorance and hardness of heart.*
> *—Ephesians 4:18*

A darkened mind leads to a hardened heart πώρωσις (*pōrōsis:* hardened or blinded) καρδōα (*kardia*: heart), the very condition that Jesus associated with the religious leadership of his day (Mark 3:5). Ultimately, this results in a life "alienated from . . . God" (Eph. 4:18).

In *Reframation: Seeing God, People, and Mission Through Reenchanted Frames* (2019), missiologists Alan Hirsch and Mark Nelson explore the "darkened frame of mind" that leads to a reduced life and a reduced church:

> *The issue is not just a loss of traditional religious faith and a declining church but a more profound loss of our whole sense of transcendence, our spiritual instincts, and our consciousness of the divine.*[94]

The church's "framing problem," which is a thinking problem, means a reduced way of understanding God, creation, other human beings, and the larger communal ecosystems that cradle the life of inherited congregations. The tragedy of a reduced life, a reduced truth, and a reduced story is conveyed in these words:

> *But here is our attempt to delve deeper, past the problems of reduced living, in order to understand that it is our reduced thinking—our theory of knowledge, how we perceive, interpret, and make sense of the world—which is at its core severely narrowed. It's not simply that the truth is reduced, but that our very way of receiving and perceiving the truth is confined.*[95]

The research of organizational expert T. K. Das confirms Hirsch and Nelson. Das demonstrates that organizations typically make mistakes in the area of perceiving their environments. Perceptions are shaped by our inner logic, and they skew our vision. Perception involves how we process and analyze basic sensory stimuli. Das shows that many strategic plans fail due to mistakes made in the early "perceiving of the environment" stage.[96]

Hirsch and Nelson write, "As we consider what it means to be human, we'd do well to note that in the New Testament, the word mind (*nous, dianoia*) constitutes 'not an instrument of thought' but 'a mode of thought' or 'mind-set.'" They further clarify this: "It therefore refers to the outlook, filter, orientation, or frames, as well as the rationale implicit" in this mindset, which is "a complex set of thoughts and assumptions which make up the consciousness of a person or their 'way of thinking.'"[97]

Ephesians 4:18 is referring, therefore, to a blinded mindset, a way of looking at the world through hard eyes, a skewed way of thinking and believing that leads to a warped way of living, alienated from God. Further, Ephesians 2:3 associates the cravings of our flesh with a darkened perception that needs cleansing for "renewing the *nous*" referred to in Romans 12:2.

Rather than a simplistic association of the language of darkness as evil and light as good, a more revealing way of describing what Paul is getting at here is that of a skewed mindset, a diminished perception, and a mind blinded to beauty, goodness, and truth. Paul instructs the church "to be renewed in the spirit of your minds, and to clothe yourselves with the new self, created according to the likeness of God in true righteousness and holiness" (Eph. 4:23–24). This renewing in the spirit of your minds opens the possibility of living a new kind of life. Or in the words of Hirsch and Nelson:

> *To translate the nous/dianoia as simply 'mind' therefore does not fully convey the biblical understanding. Rather, it approximates what we might generally call a worldview or paradigm; a particular set of frames used to view the world. And while paradigms allow us to see the world and negotiate it, they come along with what is called 'paradigm blindness.' By opting for one view of reality, the perceiver automatically deselects possible alternatives.*[98]

The Bible not only tells us *what to think about* (λογōζομαι, Phil. 4:8), it tells us *how to think* (φρονόω, Phil. 2:4). In the case of Philippians 2:4, the word φρονόω is rendered not as a noun but a verb, which evades a literal translation in the English language. It means "be minded" or to develop an attitude based on careful thought—a disposition. Hence, let the "same mind be in you that was in Jesus"—quite literally, be "Christ minded," or take on the disposition of Christ.

It may be feasible that this verse can be more fully grasped by bringing it into conversation with the concept of *habitus*, the system of schemes of thought, perception, appreciation, and action. Essentially Paul is encouraging the church to have a Jesus *habitus*.

What does this Jesus *habitus* look like? Obviously, the Bible offers some powerful examples: Mary, the mother of Jesus; Peter; Paul; Mary Magdalene; and so on. The first disciples, followers of "the way" of Jesus, earned the title "Christians," literally "little Christs." With no evangelism campaign, no professional clergy, and no dedicated buildings, the faith grew by the millions for three hundred years across the Roman Empire. It grew primarily through how the early followers lived this distinct *habitus* in a world often hostile to their faith.

But what about some historical examples? For both of us, the women who introduced us to Jesus (Len's mother and Michael's grandmother) are at the top of our list. Through the rhythms of their being, they embodied Jesus for us a in such a way that we were loved into the faith through their lives. While many people who exemplified Christlikeness throughout history get mixed reviews (mostly because they are misunderstood through the lens of presentism we will deal with later), some are universally acknowledged.

Consider Saint Thérèse of Lisieux. She lived a humble and anonymous life that had massive impact still being felt today. Her *habitus* was defined by how she did "small things with love." The life of Mother Teresa echoes through eternity for how she lived her life for others, particularly in service of the poor. Martin Luther King Jr., while known mostly for his martyrdom on the cross of the civil rights movement, embodied a nonviolent but subversive way to establish peace and equality and end segregation and discrimination across the world. His is a potent dimension of the Jesus *habitus*. Billy Graham, the evangelist to the masses, influenced millions of people, including world leaders, yet lived simply and humbly and enjoyed a scandal-free ministry spanning many decades. He embodied another dimension of the Jesus *habitus*.

Perhaps the most recent example is Pope Francis. Some would call him the most powerful man in the world, and yet he is known as a humble servant, washing the feet of the poor and the marginalized.

Philippians is a letter authored by Paul during one of his imprisonments (Phil. 1:12–14). N. T. Wright sides with interpreters that suggest it was composed in the mid-50s of the first century, less than thirty years after Jesus' execution. Many commentators agree that Philippians 2 contains a potential hymn or creedal statement that may predate Paul. Wright refers to this segment as simply a poem that potentially served as a vehicle for the early church's theology, "telling the story of both the human race and Israel, with both of them focused now on Jesus as the Messiah, Israel's representative, who is also the quintessential human being."[99]

New Testament Professor, David DeSilva notes that the voluntary humbling of Jesus in obedience to God and his exaltation to the place of greatest honor by God becomes a warrant for believers: "Paul appeals to Jesus' example specifically to curtail competition and rivalry over status within the Christian movement, showing that the precedent of Jesus was as useful for regulating relationships within the group as for strengthening the group against erosion from without."[100]

Philippians 2 has two major components: an opening statement proposing an explanation of a community of love (vv. 1–4), followed by the poem that describes the mind of Christ (vv. 5–11). In the structure of the poem itself, there is a clear contrast noticeable as two distinct trajectories: the descending of Christ (vv. 6–8), followed by an exaltation by God (vv. 9–11). The middle of the poem is the cross, the pivot point, which reverses the trajectory from descent to ascent.

Christians have been given a new mental model and a disposition that finds embodied expression in the unique *habitus* of Jesus himself. This disposition includes humility, which was not a desirable virtue in the larger Greco-Roman culture. Thus, Christians have been given a new framework through which to view reality—the very mind of Christ, which is countercultural on many levels. This is a snapshot of Jesus's own contextual intelligence.

THE MIND OF CHRIST

Philippians 2:1-11; Ephesians 4:1-24

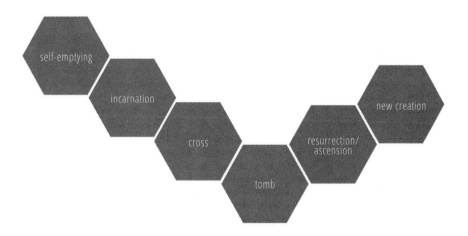

Figure 3: The Mind of Christ

We believe this framework allows us to understand and utilize contextual intelligence.

Paul implores the church community to have the "same mind . . . that was in Christ Jesus." Then he describes it step by step:

> *Let the same mind be in you that was in Christ Jesus,*
> *who, though he was in the form of God,*
> *did not regard equality with God*
> *as something to be exploited,*
> *but emptied himself,*
> *taking the form of a slave,*
> *being born in human likeness.*
> *And being found in human form,*
> *he humbled himself*
> *and became obedient to the point of death—*
> *even death on a cross.*
> *Therefore God also highly exalted him*
> *and gave him the name*
> *that is above every name,*
> *so that at the name of Jesus*
> *every knee should bend,*
> *in heaven and on earth and under the earth,*
> *and every tongue should confess*
> *that Jesus Christ is Lord,*
> *to the glory of God the Father.*
> *— Philippians 2:5–11*

As early as the fourth century, church father John Chrysostom noticed the similarities and connection between Philippians 2 and Ephesians 4. He remarks in his *Homily on Ephesians* that Paul's "design here is just the same as in the epistle to the Philippians. When he was exhorting them there he showed them Christ. So he does also here too, showing that even Christ descended to the lowest parts of the earth."[101] Jesus's incarnation is the model for all Christian behavior.

Following Chrysostom's logic, we want to draw out some parallels. The key connection point is found in what he calls the design, or, more specifically, the trajectory of descent and ascent. Philippians 2 ends with Jesus taking his seat as the glorified and enthroned Lord, yet there are more details to be fleshed out, so to speak. Ephesians 4 describes the ascending Lord gifting the church. While Jesus ascends in his resurrected body, one form of embodiment—the gifted body of Christ called the church—serves as another form of embodiment.

> *Therefore it is said,*
>
> *"When he ascended on high he made captivity itself a captive;*
>
> *he gave gifts to his people."*
>
> *(When it says, "He ascended," what does it mean but that he had also descended into the lower parts of the earth? He who descended is the same one who ascended far above all the heavens, so that he might fill all things.) The gifts he gave were that some would be apostles, some prophets, some evangelists, some pastors and teachers, to equip the saints for the work of ministry, for building up the body of Christ, until all of us come to the unity of the faith and of the knowledge of the Son of God, to maturity, to the measure of the full stature of Christ.*
>
> *—Ephesians 4:8–13*

Thus, we are linking these passages together to more fully explore the life, death, and resurrection of Jesus and the sending of the Spirit to propose a framework for the mind of Christ as a sequence of trajectories. We will now delineate the journey of the incarnation as a series of six moves.

This diagram describes each move highlighted in the passage correlated with a corresponding move in the contextual intelligence framework:

CONTEXTUAL INTELLIGENCE FRAMEWORK

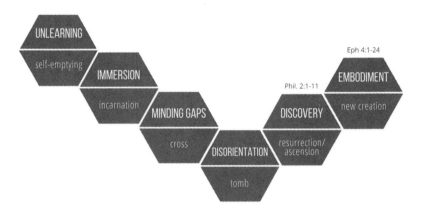

Figure 4: The Contextual Intelligence Framework

These moves could be called the *fundamentals of incarnation*—the ultimate contextualization. However, we've broken them out specifically as Paul describes them, while also filling in details from the Gospels.

The skewed mindset can be compared to faulty mental models that restrict us from attaining an accurate portrait of reality. Ephesians 4 takes place in the context of an ascended Christ, giving gifts to the church so that the body may become "fully mature in every way." How is one renewed from the diminished perceptions of a blinded mind (Eph. 4:23–24)? How does the "renewing of the *nous*" take place (Rom. 12:2)?

Paul instructs the church "to be renewed in the spirit of your minds, and to clothe yourselves with the new self, created according to the likeness of God in true righteousness and holiness" (Eph. 4:23–34). Also "to present your bodies as a living sacrifice, holy and acceptable to God, which is your spiritual worship. Do not be conformed to this world, but be transformed by the renewing of your minds, so that you may discern what is the will of God—what is good and acceptable and perfect" (Rom. 12:1–2). Finally, to "let the same mind be in you that was in Christ Jesus" (Phil. 2:5). The mind of Christ is the cleansed mind, the renewed mind, and the mind that makes the church one. The mind of Christ is embodied in our actions, a distinct Jesus *habitus*, lived out in community.

The mind of Christ is the interpretive framework that can bring clarity and understanding in a multitude of complex contexts. Remarkably, the Scriptures themselves provide this detailed framework for understanding the mind of Christ. We mean *framework* in the sense of a basic structure underlying a system or concept. Think of it as the bare frame of CQ. God has provided the undergirding structure and foundational anatomy.

Polanyi shows how in different thought paradigms, generally accepted theories can be widely held and yet remain hidden or obscure. The discovery of an *interpretive framework* can bring a new clarity and coherence to what was once a cone of confusion or a veil of uncertainty. An interpretive framework can facilitate a transformation of the intellectual life that leads to a closer relationship with reality:

Indeed, any modification of an anticipatory framework, whether conceptual, perceptual, or appetitive, is an irreversible heuristic act, which transforms our ways of thinking, aligning and attuning our beings and communities more closely to what is helpful and healing. [102]

CONTEXTUAL INTELLIGENCE FRAMEWORK

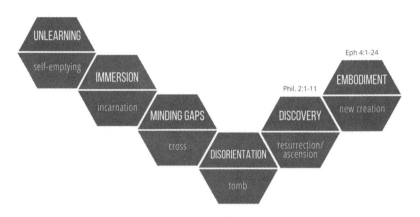

Figure 5: The Contextual Intelligence Framework (CIF)

For now, we will simply identify each of the moves and provide the theological underpinnings that will be explored in depth later. These moves will provide the sequence for the FYSAs in the following section.

(1) Self-emptying (unlearning)

The first move is about humility, "emptying self." One way to understand the significance of Jesus's self-emptying is to explore his normal development as a human being. While remaining fully God, he did indeed grow in his understanding (Luke 2:41–52). Jesus grew up in Nazareth and was called a Nazarene (Matt. 2:23), and he grew in wisdom, stature, and favor with God and humanity (Luke 2:52). Perhaps this was a kind of intentional "unlearning." The carpenter of the universe became the carpenter's son. While the mystery of the incarnation only allows us to go so far with this idea, "fully human and fully God" is an irresolvable paradox, after all. These texts demonstrate a humility in which Jesus "empties" and goes through the normal developmental process. The humility to empty, to unlearn, to embrace vulnerability, is a fundamental characteristic of the mind of Christ (Phil. 2:7–8).

For the church, contextual intelligence requires, first and foremost, humility. This emptying process includes some of our foundational assumptions as a primarily attractional, propositional, and colonial iteration of the church. Our mental models were formed in a world that is fading from view. We don't have all the answers, and we have asked wrong questions.

Thus, the first move in the contextual intelligence framework is *unlearning*: to cleanse the gates of perception; to consciously choose to give up, abandon, or stop using knowledge, values, or behaviors to acquire new ones (in the organizational sense); a process of clearing out old routines and beliefs that no longer meet current challenges.[103]

(2) Incarnation (immersion)

The second move is about vulnerability. Through the incarnation, while Jesus remains sinless, he descends into a human condition that is ultimately fallen and marred. He takes a risk. The incarnation—God coming in human flesh—is a missional endeavor. While the kingdoms of the world oppress and take captive a train of innocents in their self-seeking agendas, Jesus comes in selfless love and ultimate humiliation (crucifixion). God immerses himself fully in the context of humanity. The universal One enters into particularity. Jesus brings healing to the cosmos, not by manipulating it from the outside but through living a cruciform life in the middle of it—true contextualization.

In the North American context, Jesus's very life and death provides a model for our mission. Hence, incarnation is the form of our mission. The church as the body of Christ is an extension of the very incarnate flesh-and-blood Jesus that we proclaim, a channel of God's grace in the world.

Thus, immersion is the next move in the contextual intelligence framework: the action of immersing someone or something in a context. We must immerse ourselves in our communities in risky, vulnerable ways.

(3) Cross (minding the gaps)

The third move requires a willingness to sacrifice. Jesus willingly gives his life in the most devastating and shameful way possible. Here we see echoes of the "suffering servant" passage of Isaiah 53. There is no doubt that some of Paul's references to the form of God contrasts between humanity grasping for equality with God and Jesus self-emptying. Philippians 2 mirrors Genesis 3. Humanity takes the fruit of temptation in an attempt to be like God. Jesus, who is the very form of God, empties himself and takes on the form of sin-marred humanity to redeem the fallen condition. There is a gap between the covenant God has made with humanity and our ability to live it out. The cross is the bridge God builds across the gap. Jesus, the God-human, takes on all the forces of wickedness. On the cross, he turns human ego and violence in on itself. He himself bears our sins in his body on the cross so that, free from sins, we might live for righteousness; by his wounds you have been healed (1 Pet. 2:24).

He comes down and lives out the redemptive act that transfigures eternity. Wright, reflecting on Colossians 2, insists that in the cross, the "rulers and the powers" have been defeated through the forgiveness of sins.[104] "He disarmed the rulers and authorities and made a public example of them, triumphing over them in it" (Col. 2:15).

Jesus is the way God heals the gap.

Thus, the church is not in the self-preservation business; the church is in the self-donation business. The very eucharistic nature of the body of Christ is to break pieces of ourselves off and give them away to a hungry world.[105] Unfortunately, when our church is caught in a decline cycle, we clench our fists, desperately grasping at what's left. Yet if we open our hands and give what we are away through our own self-death, we release God to catalyze resurrection (John 12:24). Infilled by the Holy Spirit, we as the church descend into the messy brokenness of those who suffer as the hands and feet of Jesus. We stand in the tragic gaps with Jesus, bringing healing and reconciliation.

Thus, this move in the contextual intelligence framework is minding the gaps, which originates from a visual-warning phrase issued to subway riders to be careful crossing the spatial gap between the train door and the station platform. For our purposes, this is seeing the sore spots, the fragmentation, the disconnects in our community, the institutional voids where we need to sacrificially build relational bridges.

(4) Tomb (disorientation)

The fourth move requires faith and obedience in the face of uncertainty. An often-overlooked component of the incarnation is the three days that Jesus spends in the grave. God doesn't stop where we live but goes before us into death. Meeting with us in our brokenness, Jesus does not bail out when things get uncomfortable; he willingly gives his life. He trusts the Father and moves into the unknown.

Yet Romans 6:4 and Colossians 2:12 reveal not only the astonishing depths of God's love but also our place with him in the tomb. This descent into the tomb with Christ is part of our own journey to spiritual maturity. It is a move toward our own resurrection life. This inverts the modern world's values of honor, prestige, and power.

The tomb forces us into an uncomfortable state of liminality and confusion. We join the disoriented march back to our familiar Emmaus, saying, "But we had hoped that he was the one to redeem Israel. Yes, and besides all this, it is now the third day since these things took place" (Luke 24:21). The tomb represents separation, disorientation, and living in the in-between. As we carry the cross, innovate, and create new things, we hit the wall of disappointment and failure.

> *Thus, in the contextual intelligence framework, disorientation describes the state of having lost one's sense of direction and meaning. Organizationally speaking, this is living on the edge of chaos, between stagnation and innovation.*[106]

(5) Resurrection/ascension (discovery)

The fifth move is about God's supernatural intervention and how that epiphany opens our awareness to the possibility of resurrection life. In the resurrection, we discover the victory of God over sin, shame, and suffering. We see the image of the invisible God once hidden and the deep mystery now revealed that in the Christ even the Gentiles have been saved (Col. 1:24–29), something veiled since the foundation of the world (Eph. 3:1–13). It is confessing Jesus as Lord and believing God raised him from the dead, through which we are saved (Rom. 10:9).

The first Christians experienced Jesus, through the power of the Holy Spirit, as infinitely alive on both personal and communal levels (1 Cor. 12:3). It is the discovery of Christ's victory in the resurrection that humanity finds restoration from its fragmented condition. Jesus has ultimately bridged the gap as the still incarnate and risen Christ.

It wasn't until the resurrection that the disciples were transformed in their perceptions, resulting in a new mental model. In the language of Alcoholics Anonymous, they experienced *an entire psychic change*. This transformation is captured by the biblical concept of Μετανοέω: to change one's mind, to turn in another direction, a transformative change of heart, especially a spiritual conversion (eventually translated as "repent"). *Metanoia* literally means "afterthought," from *meta*, meaning "after" or "beyond," and *nous*, meaning "mind."

Resurrection = Discovery = *metanoeō*

Think of the transformation that takes place in the disciples after they encounter the risen Jesus. Mary hears him speak her name and moves from mourning to celebratory worship (John 20:16). Their "eyes were opened" to who he was in the breaking of the bread (Luke 24:31); Peter was reinstated after denial (John 21:15–17); Thomas proclaimed, "My Lord and my God!" after being invited to touch the wounds (John 20:24–29); and so on. Their concepts of the Messiah, from conquering king to crucified and now risen Lord went through a metamorphosis based on the discovery of the resurrection. Up until Jesus's arrest and even beyond to the reports of the empty tomb, they continued to misunderstand who he was. In his resurrected body, he opens the Scriptures to them (Luke 24:27) and gifts them with the Holy Spirit (John 20:19–23). Through these encounters, they become entirely different people.

Peter Senge defines *metanoia* as simply "real learning," the kind that gets to the heart of being human. This is a radical shift in awareness, the fundamental shift of mind. The kingdom of God is at hand, but you need a shift of mind to see it. He goes on to say that "learning is leading."[107]

Metanoia is an unending process of unlearning, learning, and relearning. We need shifts in our ecological, social, political, economic, emotional, relational, and spiritual understanding. Discovery transitions us into knowing what to do.

Thus, in the contextual intelligence framework, this move is described as discovery, the action or process of attaining new insight. New discoveries lead to innovation. Once we move through the process of liminality and disorientation, our reality can be transformed. However, if the discovery is not scaled or downloaded and spread throughout the system, it fails. This leads us to the final move: embodiment.

(6) New Creation (embodiment):

The final move is about a new form of embodiment, ranging from a transformed *habitus* individually to the formation of a new communal manifestation of Jesus's life. Taking this journey may lead to a new you, a new ministry, a new contextual Christian community, and so on. Philippians 2 envisions an ascended Lord, surrounded by a new communal embodiment consisting of every knee and every tongue bent and confessing "in heaven and on earth and under the earth," heralding a transformation that is cosmic in scope. Philippians 3:17–4:1 envisions the mature community living a resurrected life now with our citizenship already in heaven.

Ephesians 4 further informs the meaning of the ascension for this new colony of heaven on earth. The resurrected body of Jesus on the throne is not the only body. Jesus has a body on the earth as well—the church. The church is filled and gifted by the Spirit. Jesus, the head of the church, has given us the mind of Christ. He who fills all things (Eph. 4:10) and who has poured out his Spirit on all people (Acts 2:14–21) is bringing the healing of the cosmos (Rom. 8:19–23).

For better or worse, the gifts God gives to the church is us—gifted persons (Eph. 4:10–11). An embodied and gifted community called the church is God's missional instrument on the earth.

> *Thus, the final move of the contextual intelligence framework is described as embodiment, the tangible or visible form of an idea, quality, or, in our case, a person. The mind of Christ is now embodied in a community.*

As the contextual intelligence framework is a journey of increasing Jesus' embodiment, we now offer you a palette of competencies that can be observed and cultivated in the form of a palette of FYSAs.

CHAPTER 11

PALETTE OF FYSAS

Core Competencies of a High CQ

CONTEXTUAL INTELLIGENCE FRAMEWORK

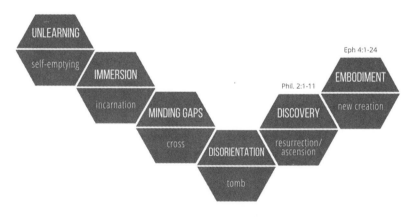

Diseases have a character of their own, but they also partake of our character; we have a character of our own, but we also partake of the world's character . . . the disease—the person—the world go together, and cannot be considered separately as things-in-themselves.

—Oliver Sacks[108]

A palette is a thin board on which an artist lays and mixes colors. These competencies are like the core colors that can help you grow in the art of reading your context and knowing what to do.

The intelligence community deploys an acronym, FYSA, which stands for "For Your Situational Awareness." The military often uses FYSAs to help troops become aware of their context. This enables soldiers to self-organize their responses and make better decisions in the face of contextual variations on the battlefield. In combat, situational awareness is crucial. An accurate understanding of one's surroundings can be a matter of life and death. This is usually true of churches as well.

An incarnational relationship with context is more than a "situationship" but less than a marriage. *Situationship* refers to an unsteady, undependable relationship. No missionary would declare their calling to a mission field a situationship with God. The Pilgrims, for example, did not consider their mission to the New World to be based on a situationship with God.

Every context is a drama of deixis and situationality. Contextual intelligence is the art of understanding current conditions. It involves putting people in their place, but not in a negative way. When people embrace a posture of placefulness, it is something to celebrate, especially when their place is their place of origination,[109] or ordination, or ordinance and ordnance.

In the network society, *deterritorialization* describes the disconnection from geography in a digital world. As we live in the space of real virtuality, hyperconnected by the screens of our tech devices, we become dislocated from our neighborhoods. The COVID-19 pandemic caused us to hunker down and practice social distancing but simultaneously forced us to stay in our place. In many cases, we had forgotten that physical space was even there, but exhaustion from the constant fixation on our anxiety-inducing screens caused us to take walks, look around, see our place again.

When the regional becomes the regal, you live your zip code, love your zip code, pray your zip code, and eat and breathe your zip code. We hope these will help you do that.

Palette of FYSAs

Core Competencies of a High CQ

CONTEXTUAL INTELLIGENCE FRAMEWORK
THE MIND OF CHRIST: Philippians 2:1-11; Ephesians 4:1-24

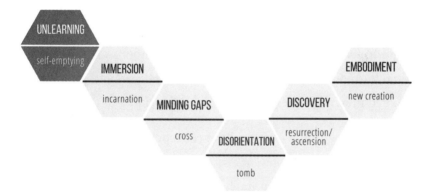

FYSA #1: Unlearning

The illiterate of the twenty-first century will not be those who cannot read or write but those who cannot learn, unlearn, and relearn.

—Alvin Toffler

The major biblical word for a Jesus disciple is the Greek *mathétés*, which translates as "follower or disciple or learner or student." All followers of Jesus are learners. "Learn from me," Jesus said (Matt. 24:32–33). Hence, Jesus's response, "You do not yet understand" (Matt. 16:2–3). Discipleship means lifelong learning of faith seeking understanding, which requires the church to be not just a community of practice but a community of learning. But the flip side of learning is unlearning. The church is a community of both learning and unlearning.

Knowledge-Wisdom-Truth: All learning moves from knowledge to wisdom to truth. All knowledge begins with a realization: "I don't know my way about." All wisdom requires trifocals: learning the lens of understanding what happened in the past, learning the lens of perceiving what is happening now, and learning the lens of refashioning a new future. All truth begins with a recognition of Jesus as life's best guide.

Success cannot be replicated in another context without adaptation to the context. Every success must be achieved and every game won on its own terms and in its own context. Success means unlearning what we think we know and learning the immediate context with fresh ears and eyes. Children transplanted in new cultures innately take on this skill.

A daily challenge in life is to shed the conceptual shackles that bind and confine our thinking and prevent us from experiencing God. Cartoonist/playwright Lynda Barry has a graphic essay, "Two Questions," where she defines play as "not knowing long enough for something alive to take shape." That's the essence of unlearning—to risk not knowing or knowing wrong so that the Spirit can bring to life something that "takes shape" in original, contextualized form.

The core competency of contextual intelligence of unlearning[110] is what keeps us from straying off the path of wisdom and understanding. Unlearning is what keeps the body of Christ pregnant with new life and hope for the future.

> *To look at something as though we had never seen it before requires great courage.*
>
> —*Henri Matisse*

"Have you understood all this?" Jesus asked his disciples. They nodded yes (Matt. 13:51). At best, we should nod to the cross, "Yes and no." We all understand at best in part, and our best understanding is always subject to addenda and corrigenda (errors to be corrected). All the more so when it comes to such "all this" as the incarnation. If theoretical physicist Richard Feynman (1918–1988) could admit, "Nobody understands quantum mechanics; if you think you do, you don't," how much more do we not understand this one word *Emmanuel* or *God with us* or the nature of faith itself?

First of all, we know too many things that are wrong, which leads us to want the wrong things.

First of all, we know too many things that are wrong, which leads us to want the wrong things. We learn in ways we don't understand, and our thinking is shaped by contexts without and contexts within that bias us to see what we want to see, to read our own agendas into our context, and to overreach rather than receive only what our context is offering.

> *Let us take what the terrain gives.*
>
> *—maxim of cognitive scientist Amos Tversky (1937–1996)*

Much of our learning comes from inner yearnings or outer hearsay (and hates), from which we make assumptions that misunderstand other cultures. For example, Hindu culture is misunderstood in the word *pariah*, which actually means "ritual drummer," not "outcast," as we have adopted into English. In a world where all too often two sides willfully or through ignorance or mischief misrepresent and misunderstand what the other is saying, learning is harder than ever, especially when neither side makes any real effort to understand the other.

Second, we know too many things that are wrong for the world we're in. Just when you think you really understand something, inconsistencies and incontinences happen to totally upend your understanding and reveal your ignorance. We have to unlearn our hard-learned, hard-earned, hard-eyed assumptions to see the world as it is as if for the first time. The unlearning competency discards quickly our surety of knowing. Our communities need to be unlearning communities so they can become learning communities.

In a post-Christendom scenario, we have experienced a change of ecosystems. Congregational consultant Gil Rendle refers to the season in which the US church flourished as an "aberrant time." The sociocultural amalgamation in which the church as we know it was planted was an aberration.[111] The conditions that caused Christendom to thrive in the United States, largely corporate iterations of attractional, propositional, and colonial models, are no longer true. This is not a technical problem with a technical solution. This is an adaptive challenge that forces us to learn to live in an entirely new ecosystem. The church planted in jungle conditions, lush with low-hanging fruit, must now learn how to live in a desert.

If you think you understand, it isn't God.

—*Søren Kierkegaard*

A way to approach understanding this is through the phenomenon of wicked versus kind learning environments. Robin Hogarth et al. describe *wicked learning environments* as "situations in which feedback in the form of outcomes of actions or observations is poor, misleading, or even missing." In contrast, *kind learning environments* are ones in which "feedback links outcomes directly to the appropriate actions or judgments and is both accurate and plentiful."[112]

In the institutional voids, the rules change. In the church, clergy are being trained as specialists in a world of generalists.[113] Most of our education is preparing us for a kind learning environment. In the local church, we assume clergy are being deployed to a fairly uniform experience, like a chess game. We know the board; we know how the pieces move, we know what it takes to win.

For instance, in the United Methodist Church, elders are ordained (after a rigorous screening process) to a ministry of Word, Sacrament, Order, and Service. Elders preach and teach, administer the sacraments, order the life of the church, and serve the congregants and community. These essential roles can be expressed in a multitude of environments in an endless array of contextual variations. Yet those roles also carry a set of Christendom assumptions—that there will be congregants, for one. Increasingly, clergy are deployed to settings where the number of congregants is dwindling, where unceasing church fights resemble two bald men fighting over a comb, and where the respect for and support of professional clergy are often problematic.

The Western educational paradigm is deficient in cultivating an understanding of contextual and cultural variation. Every church is a unique context, and a degree of adaptation will always be necessary. But clergy now encounter wicked problems in wicked domains in a post-Christendom culture, where acquired learning does not have a linear progression to assumed predictions and expected perks.

Propositional knowledge is knowledge of truths or facts; non-propositional knowledge includes practical knowledge, and the kind of understanding provided by art which shows things it does not say.

—*Oxford philosopher A. W. Moore*[114]

Does experience always lead to expertise? Of course not. It depends to a large degree on the domain in question. Inference involves reaching a conclusion on the basis of evidence. Yet inference must take place in an actual environment. At the simplest level, the process involves two settings:

1. Information is acquired (learning)

2. Information is applied (predictions or choices)

However, the environment will shape the outcomes. Kind learning environments "involve close matches between the informational elements in the two settings and are a necessary condition for accurate inferences," while wicked learning environments involve "mismatches."[115] This conceptual framework allows us to identify sources of inferential errors. It can also provide a means to target corrective procedures and maximize behavior. In other words, context matters. It influences how the 1 Chronicles 12:32 process of "understanding the times" and "knowing what to do" will unfold.

While Hogarth's study is primarily concerned with pinpointing the sources of errors between such things as task structure and the persons involved, we can make some obvious correlations with church ecosystems.

Kind learning environments

Patterns repeat consistently. Feedback is accurate and rapid. (Thus, deliberative practice, instinctive pattern recognition, and narrow, repetitive experiences are needed for mastery.)

Wicked learning environments

May not include repetitive patterns. Rules of the game are unclear. Status quo changes. Feedback is often delayed, inaccurate, or both. (Thus, range of skills, applying knowledge from one pursuit creatively to another, adaptation, and outside experience are needed for mastery.)[116]

For people trained in kind learning environments, being deployed to wicked learning environments is like being trained as a classical musician only to be launched into outer space as an astronaut. It requires significant adaptation and the ability to learn the new environment. Contextual adaption requires applying relevant knowledge and jettisoning irrelevant knowledge. This is true for every church in every community. Yet this reality is even more pronounced due to the level of societal and cultural change in the United States. Every church is now a wicked learning environment.

Furthermore, a person taking actions based on false inferences can *create* a wicked learning environment. For example, a clergy person who has a track record of serving declining congregations uses the same old methods at a new church, and once again decline results. A kind of self-fulfilling prophecy. Another clergy person with a history of serving growing congregations employs the same tried-and-true methods, and this congregation declines. Their actions are guided by a range of data from past experiences but fail to understand the variations of the environment.

Only those thoughts are true which do not understand themselves.

—*German philosopher/psychologist Theodor Adorno (1903–1969)*

A group of church leaders in a declining congregation receive a new pastor. They are convinced their decline is because of the last three pastors' ineffectiveness. They enculturate the new pastor into their program, but the decline continues. Again, they are triggering the mismatch by basing their predictions on faulty assumptions. They are creating a wicked environment by basing inferences and actions on data that is not reliable or valid.

You will never know your context as well as a spider knows its web, manipulating your zip code like a spider maintaining its domain. Nor should you. Because your web is changing its netting and threading all the time. Contexts consistently change, which means understanding a context is less like watching the clock and more like observing cloud formations, as Robert

Service has memorialized in the gorgeous metaphor "Cultures are more like clouds than clocks." [117]

Just when we have an accurate picture of the cloud, environmental variables create changes. The formations are always responding to the evanescent conditions of moisture, atmospheric pressure, and so on. Contextual intelligence involves a continuous process of learning and unlearning—taking in new data, getting rid of old data, and then basing predictions and choices on that new data.

Those who cannot remember the past are condemned to repeat it. To covet truth is a very distinguished passion.

—philosopher/novelist George Santayana (1863–1952)

Unlearning hurts. Discarding obsolete knowledge and reflecting critically on our failures is painful. Perhaps this is why we can't do it . . . sometimes even if our lives are dependent on it.

In 1934, Dr. William D. Silkworth was the medical director of Towns Hospital, New York, NY. He began to notice that the problem of alcoholism was centered in the mind, manifesting as an allergy that unleashed a phenomenon of craving. Once an alcoholic took a single drink, the allergy was unleashed. Confessing the frustrations of his failed treatments, he encountered an anomaly—a case of the most extreme variety—that had now seemingly recovered from a hopeless state of mind and body. This individual, a positive deviant, was now helping other alcoholics recover in a rapidly growing fellowship. [118]

Silkworth wrote of alcoholics, "Unless this person can experience an entire psychic change, there is very little hope of recovery," and the new ideals of these individuals must be grounded in a "power greater than themselves." [119] The individual he treated was Bill W., cofounder of Alcoholics Anonymous, a now global fellowship of more than two million people, including 180 nations and more than 118,000 AA groups around the world.[120]

This thriving, global, leaderless organization, which has saved many millions of lives, is founded on some very simple principles. These principles are crystallized in the collective intelligence of AA members everywhere in the form of recovery fellowship clichés, such as "I don't have a drinking problem; I have a thinking problem." Simultaneously, this is held in tension with another cliché, "I can't think my way into sober living, but I can live my way into sober thinking." Alcoholics learn a new set of behaviors—praying, going to meetings, talking to a sponsor, reading the "big book," and making coffee. As we "fake it till we make it," we live ourselves into a new mindset, an "entire psychic change."

One of the foundational principles of AA is unlearning. Alcoholics must go through a process of changing "people, places, and things" and embracing a new mental model, an "entire psychic change." Our lives depend on this... but it hurts. This is fundamentally true of churches as well.

A 2018 experiment published in the *Journal of Experimental Psychology* demonstrated that unlearning was essential in interventions for drug abuse and other maladaptive habitual behaviors. In fact, it showed that if unlearning does not occur, interventions "may yield temporary success but are often fragile and relapse is common." Many interventions failed because they were ineffective at erasing or substantially modifying the representations that facilitated the "underlying addictive behavior—that is, they do not cause true unlearning."[121]

The study also showed that relapse often occurred when addicts returned to the original context of their drug use. This is partly true because many interventions occur in clinics. In the sanitized context of a clinic, the addict learned new clinic-specific associations. However, the addiction-driving stimulus-response associations were not actually affected. Addicts unlearn the clinic-specific associations upon reentry into complexities of the original context of the drug abuse.[122] Context is queen indeed, but Jesus is king.

Both positive and negative behaviors can be learned and are not easily unlearned. An intervention is an attempt to disrupt this destructive behavior cycle. The secret of the Issacharians is an intervention for the Eurotribal church. But just as every recovering person knows, recovery is predicated on a relationship with a "power greater than ourselves." The Jesus who can heal the sick and raise the dead can give us the power to unlearn as well.

The military has a motto: "It's better to learn than be dead." A variation of this is true for the church as well: "It's better to unlearn than be closed."

No one can possibly know what is about to happen: It is happening, each time, for the first time, for the only time.

—*novelist James Baldwin (1924–1987)*

CONTEXTUAL INTELLIGENCE FRAMEWORK
THE MIND OF CHRIST: Philippians 2:1-11; Ephesians 4:1-24

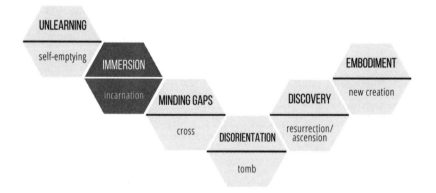

FYSA #2: See the Self-Evident

You see, but you do not observe.

—*Sherlock Holmes to Dr. Watson*

One of the hardest things in life is to see what is right in front of us. Nothing is quite as it seems. There is always more there. Just as we can miss the obvious, we can miss the spaces, the silences, the "what isn't there" that often is as important as what is there.

To observe clearly the obvious and to state clearly the conspicuous is the most demanding of contextual feats. We are oblivious to the obvious. We prefer the airy abstractions that horoscope writers love so well to the gritty, grimy details of the streets. We have become suspicious readers that look for the latent depths and dismiss or glide over the surface shallows.

In other words, a surface reading is a positive imperative. Sometimes that which is evident, perceptible, and apprehensible, which respects rather than rejects what is in plain view, is the hardest of readings. If you're having trouble seeing, shut your eyes and Braille the culture. Get a feel for it first, and then open your eyes to see what you feel. Every context is lush and verdant, full of vibrant colors and teeming with life if you open your eyes and pay attention.

Jesus taught his disciples to be canaries in the coal mine, to hone their competencies in contextual intelligence. One aspect of this was learning to read the signs, or σημεον (*semeion*), of the times.

> *"From the fig tree learn its lesson: as soon as its branch becomes tender and puts forth its leaves, you know that summer is near. So also, when you see all these things, you know that he is near, at the very gates."*

> — *Matthew 24:32–33*

Jesus lambasted the Pharisees for their unfitness in sign-reading:

> *"When it is evening, you say, 'It will be fair weather, for the sky is red.' And in the morning, 'It will be stormy today, for the sky is red and threatening.' You know how to interpret the appearance of the sky, but you cannot interpret*

the signs of the times."

— Matthew 16:2–3

"Hypocrites! You know how to interpret the appearance of the earth and the sky. How is it that you don't know how to interpret this present time?"

— Luke 12:56

Fourteen times in the Gospels and three times in Revelation, Jesus directly tells his disciples, or implies in his teaching, to "watch" (*grēgoreō*): give strict attention to, be cautious, actively pay attention. One of Jesus's trademark sayings is "He who has ears," the equivalent of "Listen up! Pay close attention!" He is quoted saying this six times in the Gospels and eight times in Revelation, a phrase that is close to another signature phrase, perhaps even his favorite, that means basically the same thing and peppers almost every page of the Gospels: "I tell you the truth," or in today's language, "Pay attention."

Pay attention to the cultural codes and conventions. Pay attention to who is getting pulled over by the PC culture cops and failing their sobriety tests. They are most often voices of the past but frequently enough voices of the future that you ignore at your peril. Pay attention to tinctures of text, texture, taste, *terroir*, and contaminants. Every age is tinctured by time. Every age is tainted by time. What's the tincture? What's contaminated?

Tinctures of Text

A tincture refers to a slight trace of something. CQ involves following the traces and clues in texts. Pioneering English novelist Virginia Woolf (1882–1941) said the great themes of literature are "love and battle and jealousy." The great themes of the Bible (besides the one authoritative theme of Jesus) are sin and grace (salvation), evil and suffering, covenant (relationship) and creation, shalom (kingdom) and love. Read and scan the culture around you for those themes at work and at play in your midst.

Stacks and Stars are two of the most inspiring places to check and check-in: the stacks of a library and the stars of heaven. What are the people in your context reading? Are they reading? How bright are the stars, or is there so much air pollution and light pollution that the stars are hidden in the darkness?

Observe and consider the cultural codes and conventions, the canons of correctness, whether political, theological, or emotional. The original introduction to *Animal Farm* (1945), never published in George Orwell's lifetime, included this warning:

> *At any given moment there is an orthodoxy, a body of ideas which it is assumed that all right-thinking people will accept without question. It is not exactly forbidden to say this, that or the other, but it is 'not done' to say it, just as in mid-Victorian times it was 'not done' to mention trousers in the presence of a lady. Anyone who challenges the prevailing orthodoxy finds himself silenced with surprising effectiveness.* [123]

It's these very cultural "orthodoxies" that a few decades later are the lambasts and laughingstocks of the future.

Distinguish between morals and ethics. Ethics have to do with "ought-ness"; morals have to do with "is-ness." Ethics are normative; morals are descriptive. In an ideal setting, the higher the ethical standard, the higher the moral behavior. But when ethics and morals are confused (as is the case in Western civilization), then the way things are (morals) becomes the way things ought to be (ethics).

Fables are profound stories, the deep truths of *mythos* that express themselves in *logos* and *ethos*. Fables are the green pastures where our beings are "re-storied." What stories are they telling? What images are they using? What are the master metaphors and mother narratives?

Drawing out people's stories is an acquired skill in a Post-it culture. We live in a porn world of posts. But reading posts is a world apart from listening to stories. Exchanging stories takes forbearance, restraint, sensitivity, attentiveness, trust, mutuality, subtlety. Impersonal, impulsive posting is porn. Exchanging stories is romance.

Want to get back home? Shetland fishermen in the northern isles of Scotland used to claim they used the *moder dy*—the mother wave—to steer them back to Shetland. Good contextual intelligence is not living with a mother wave but the right mother story that can chart our course through difficult, choppy waters. Every context has a mother story and master metaphor, both of which are often cocooned in a soundtrack. What songs are they singing and playing? The mother stories, master metaphors, and maestro soundtracks tell you most of what you need to know.

There are five story dynasties in Western culture, five bodies of lore that galvanize us and gather us together: Harry Potter (seven story arcs), Game of Thrones (eight seasons, seventy-one episodes), Lord of the Rings (six books in Tolkien's original structure), the Marvel Universe (twenty-two story arcs), and Star Wars (nine movies, with three more coming). Only with a high CQ can you make the Jesus Story (sixty-six story arcs) the most scintillating structure in your narrative universe.

Jesus is the central story of each of the sixty-six books of the Bible. Jesus taught the disciples to follow the traces of himself throughout the narrative universe of their sacred Scriptures: "Then beginning with Moses and all the prophets, he interpreted to them the things about himself in all the scriptures"

(Luke 24:27). If we look closely at the five story dynasties in Western culture, we will find the golden thread of Jesus as well. Contextually intelligent Jesus followers know how to enter those stories, pull out the gold, and showcase it to others. This requires us to enter the story of others, to communicate in their native stories, and to point to the Jesus who is already there.

Why are stories of our coming together and healing not as interesting as stories of our falling apart and breaking down? The very word Jesus, or Yeshuah, means "God saves" or "God heals." What are the saving and healing stories in your context? There are so many beautiful things in this world. How much beauty do we miss? How much rainbow dust in your midst are you failing to appreciate?

Stories are what made the past, and stories are what will make the future. That's why the best answer to bad theology is good story, not good theology. The bottom line is a storyline, not a financial document. Don't trust accounting spreadsheets. Trust storylines and soundtracks.

> *If you want to change people's conduct, you need to change their imagination.*
> *—French philosopher Paul Ricoeur (1913–2005)*

Sometimes the context needs a paradigm shift. Sometimes the paradigm doesn't need to shift but just be problematized and reframed with new metaphors and narratives. How do you navigate a world of constant turbulence, negotiate cascading avalanches of information and chicanes of alternative facts and fake news? You use the GPS of narrative. Business has become better at crafting, correcting, and communicating narratives of mission and vision than the church. Corporations and their managerial troubadours have colonized storytelling to the point that *tell* and *sell* mean the same thing. Facebook has bet the farm on stories, wooing advertisers to adopt story-framed pitches and tailor them to spread across Instagram,

Messenger, WhatsApp and Twitter.

Here are some triggers for your tracking in seeing the self-evident:

- **Stables.** Triggers for your tracking: What are the immutables, dependables, unknowables, intractables, durables, incurables, respectables, irrefutables?

- **Observables.** Triggers for your tracking: What are the fashionables, indispensables, vulnerables, measurables, questionables, untouchables, unavoidables, communicables, accountables, uncomfortables, sociables, implacables, formidables (strengths)?

- **Notables.** Triggers for your tracking: What are the admirables, memorables, valuables, veritables, favorables, remarkables, quotables, pleasurables, capables, unbelievables, unevadables, unforgettables, adorables?

- **Unpredictables.** Triggers for your tracking: In history's march to the future, the foreseen is seldom seen or realized. The unforeseen is. Wild cards and black swans lurk around every corner. What are the wild cards, unstables, ineffables, inflammables? Unpredictable is not the same as capricious. To say that God is unpredictable is not to say that God is capricious or impulsive.

There are some predictable unpredictables. Every pastor knows what it means to settle into a "troubled seas" default. When days are quiet and serene, one still braces, knowing it's the calm before the storm. There is always a storm coming. Every disciple and church should learn this "troubled seas" default.

- **Objectionables**: Triggers for your tracking: What are the miserables, unspeakables, debatables, unbearables, unconscionables, despicables, lamentables, inexcusables, unreliables, unfathomables, indecipherables, irritables, intolerables?

Tinctures of Texture

Braille the culture (e.g., "feel" the bumps and bruises, the cracks and crevices). What is the EQ of the place and space?

> *Don't tell me to look at something. I have to close my eyes to see what's really there.*
>
> *—Woodcarver's Motto*

Where do you find outcroppings and outflowings of life's most powerful emotions—fear, grief, courage, love?

Vox populi is not *vox dei*. But we need to hear the voices of the people. Besides, something can be a lie and still speak cultural truth.

What hits you like a punch in the mouth?

What impacts you like a kiss on the lips?

Tinctures of Taste

Disciples with high CQs also have a high missional consciousness. Missional is not a winning or a conquering but an invitation to a feast and festival—a feast in the kingdom of God (Luke 14:16). All mission must be "mission in Christ's way" . . . which means it is kenotic, self-giving, humble, sacrificial, loving, and forgiving.

Missional churches and missional disciples ("missional churches/disciples" is a *pleonasm*, meaning the use of multiple words that mean the same thing) are those who notify people they have an invitation to a banquet, to a feast, to a table—an invitation that is extended first and foremost to "the poor, the crippled, the blind and the lame" (Luke 14:21).

Family is formed and forged and friendships are made and matured around tables. All tables are good, but home tables and church tables are best. A Facebook culture requires more facetime and mealtime, not less. Barriers generally fall in face-to-face laughing and looking in each other's eyes. But nothing builds bonds more than facetime at mealtimes. In the Emmaus Road story, the phrase "They were kept from seeing him" is another way of saying that words are not enough to see Jesus. We need food, we need faith, and we need the table and the conversation over the table after the meal is over, which goes by the name of *sobremesa* ("over the table").

- How important is the table at your church and in your community? (By *table*, we mean both the Lord's Table and the food table.)

- Where do people gather to eat, and how do they gather?

- Are your family and your church outsourcing your table or hosting it?

- Do people gather at various locations just to eat and drink, or do they have times and places where they gather to eat and drink together?

- In your church, how important is the common table, or the sacrament of Communion?

- Do you have a common table, a table where the community can gather for the Communion of sacramental togethering?

- Are people gathering, or are they togethering?

- Listen to the Jesse Colin Young song "Get Together."[124]

- How multicultural and multiclass is the togethering at the table?

Plutarch, in his *Table Talk* (c. AD 100), says, "Do not invite one another merely to eat and drink, but to eat and drink together." Jesus promised to be present "where two or three gather together" (Matt. 18:20). It's not in the eating, drinking, and gathering but in the eating, drinking and gathering *together*. There is no true gathering without togethering, which may be the very best definition of *sobremesa*.

> *There are two symbols, bread and money; and there are two mysteries, the eucharistic mystery of bread and the Satanic mystery of money. We are faced with the great task: to overthrow the rule of money and to establish in its place the rule of bread.*
>
> —*Russian theologian Nicholas Berdyaev*[125]

When Christians celebrate, they say it in grain (bread) and grape (wine). What does grain and grape say about your own community?

Tinctures of Terroir

Find the unique taste of the culture. For instance, the *terroir* (French— from medieval Latin *territorium*) refers to the totality of texts, textures, and tastes.

Every context has a *terroir*, a unique taste, a one-of-a-kind flavor, a somewhereness. This term refers primarily to the natural environment of grapes in which a particular wine is produced. Cumulative factors such as soil, topography, and climate contribute to the *terroir*. The characteristics of a wine's taste are imparted by the contextual factors that led to its production. *Terroir* is about a somewhereness. What is unique about your context? What is the somewhereness of your community? This *terroir* of your context cannot be experienced by reading statistical reports or asking others. You immerse yourself in the context in order to taste the somewhereness for yourself. Immersion requires utilizing all the senses.

Tinctures of Contaminants

This is about ferreting out and naming the evils of the culture.

Every context is tainted. Every culture is corrupted. Identify the bugs and viruses and corruptions. Last place to look for good critiques of context and culture? Philosophers and intellectuals (ivory towers). Best first ports-of-call? Artists and chefs, who know best the dirty streets and hungry hearts.

Remember the hard truth that the assumptions and jargon of the day, the buzzwords, orthodoxies, and PC phrases, will be in the future the very things most critiqued and lambasted.

Contaminants are the sore spots where healing is needed. There is soreness in every context. In every community there exist populations of the hungry, marginalized, or lonely. In the emerging economic reality of the United States, the massive unbalanced distribution of wealth has diminished the existence of the middle class that was once the primary volunteer base of churches—what Paul Taylor calls "a hollowing of the middle."[126] This is a big gap. Why are churches still targeting a middle class that largely no longer exists when so many American families visit food banks and live below the poverty line?

Although prevalent, poverty is not always the only kind of soreness.

Although prevalent, poverty is not always the only kind of soreness. Every community is sore and tainted in some way. Even in affluent communities, there is some ache that God desires to heal. The Villages, Florida, is a retirement community called "Florida's Friendliest Hometown." Some think this pristine gated community would be absent of typical sinfulness elsewhere. This is a false assumption. One of our churches (Michael), Wildwood UMC, is located on the edge of this rapidly growing city. We have recovery meetings every day of the week. This is a soft place to land "outside the bubble" (as Villagers refer to it) for those struggling with various issues.

Thus, one of our ministries takes place on the edge, in the shadows, amidst the dark underbelly of The Villages. Prostitution, alcoholism, and addiction are prevalent just below the well-polished surface. Further, divorce, death, abandonment, and loneliness exist in all communities. This is a sore community, but in a different way. The greatest soreness in a network society is isolation. People are connected in blazing 5G speed all the time and yet isolated, longing for authentic connection.

This is what the Fall is about, the shattering of relationships that leave one alone—the contaminant. Within this scenario, the church can offer the world the greatest gift of all. In fact, the only gift we can offer, no other organization can—communal life with Jesus. The life that heals our isolation.

After Jesus's resurrection, all the disciples had trouble recognizing him. It's still our problem. But if we have trouble recognizing the face of Jesus, missing the face of beauty, goodness, and truth all around us, how much more do we miss or misread the face of evil? Look for the manifold faces of evil in your context: vanishing values, family breakdown, youth crime and gangs, consumerism, drugs and alcohol abuse, racism, trafficking, climate change, habitat destruction, greed, graft, fishery practices, etc.

Graham Cray, bishop of the Church of England and godfather of the Fresh Expressions movement, and his team had the CQ to see the self-evident. They recognized the church as we know it was no longer connecting with most people and that churches could not be planted fast enough to make up the rate at which they were closing. They were first-class noticers, who saw the need for "Fresh Expressions of church" in the Church of England, which they promoted in the *Mission-Shaped Church* report of 2004. They saw the need for contextual forms of church to reach the growing mass of "nones and dones." The rest is history, as Fresh Expressions are now springing up all over the world.[127]

CONTEXTUAL INTELLIGENCE FRAMEWORK

THE MIND OF CHRIST: Philippians 2:1-11; Ephesians 4:1-24

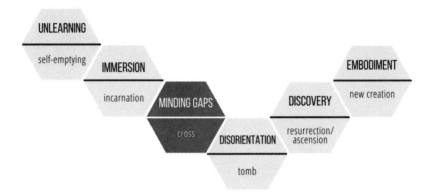

FYSA #3: Tracking and Trailing

When we view people, places, circumstances, and events with "soft eyes," we move through a kind of transformation where we discover a reality that was always there, but which we missed. We discover a reality that can shift the way we relate to people, solve problems, face challenges and live life—at work, at home, at play, and in relationship.

—Peter Vajda

Two of humanity's oldest pursuits are an evening activity and a morning quest. The evening activity is telling stories around the glow of a campfire. The morning quest is tracking and trailing in the savannah after the evening storytelling. The two are related in that you tell at nighttime what you tracked in the morning. In the morning, you are a story catcher. In the evening, you are a storyteller.

Moderns lost the ability to do both: track and tell. Even indigenous peoples, who were known as the best animal trackers and story keepers, lost the skills of both. We are now in the midst of a massive revival of these two lost arts: tracking and storytelling. Indigenous peoples all over the world are hiring trackers to teach them tracking. The native bushmen of Botswana hired world-renowned tracker Adrian to teach them how to track in Africa. Many Native American tribes, without any tradition of tracking, are only now hiring African trackers to teach them the ways of their ancestors. Few conferences are on more bucket lists than storytelling festivals. Graphicacy (digital literacy) has brought with it a revival of oracy (oral culture).

Some years ago, SpiritVenture Ministries (SVM) decided to bring these two lost arts—nature tracking and storytelling—into one African "Advance." SVM hired Callie Roos, a renowned tracker of the Big Five game in Africa, to show how to track wild animals on the ground at the Timbavati game reserve in South Africa. At the same time, Len provided theological riffs on how to spot and track the Holy Spirit in the wilds of our postmodern culture. In the words of semiotics founder Charles Sanders Peirce, "We must not begin by talking pure ideas—vagabond thoughts that tramp the public highways without any human habitation—but must begin with people and their conversation."

After Roos showed evidence of how animals sometimes track us when we think we are tracking them, we showed how the Hound of Heaven is often on our tracks, hunting and haunting us with the love of God and wooing us to holy life. The Spirit is seeking to bring us from our hiding places into the light of God's presence, tracking us. But to track the Spirit is one of the greatest skills of contextual intelligence.

Culture is a language and a landscape. Learning to read that language and landscape we have lost the skill to read is what is called semiotics. Everyone does semiotics. The only issue is how well and how consciously do we do it.

In the not-too-distant past, and still today in certain parts of the world, one's survival depended upon the ability to read your environment—specifically, the signs that tracked one's dinner. The most obvious tracker's signs might be footprints in the mud, snow, or sand, scat, discarded food, claw scarring, and trails through the forest or jungle. Less obvious signs might be overturned stones and stunted vegetation.[128] The tracker's ability to read these signs can speak volumes about where the subject has been, what it has been doing, where it is going, and, more importantly, what it is following.[129]

While most of us today are not scanning savannahs in search of sustenance, we are quite adept at traversing the economic terrain in search of those items that might satisfy our multiple hungers. Biologist Carol Yoon suggests these ancient tracking skills have been repurposed for the new environment in which we now find ourselves.[130] In essence, we are still hunter-gatherers; we are just no longer tracking animals in their natural habitat but instead are maneuvering ourselves to aisle seven in our preferred grocery garden.

We track the mind of God in the footsteps of Jesus. We touch the Father's heart in the wounds of the Son. In medieval devotion, the five wounds of Jesus on the cross symbolized the five broken places and senses of the human species—wounds of touch, sight, hearing, scent, and taste.[131] These are the primary sign-reading tools we use in life, the forest, or the marketplace: sight, sound, smell, taste, touch. When combined with time, they provide life with something called experience.

Trackers of *Vestigia Trinitatis*

In all that exists, you can find what the early church called *vestigia Trinitatis*, or "footprints of the Trinity." God is omnipresent, present in the mundane, the arcane and the macabre. The footprints of the Trinity are most apparent in those three things that bring wellness and wholeness to the world: community, mystery, and beauty.

Consider this book your enrollment in a tracking school for those footprints of the Trinity and your first course in trinitarian tracking.[132] If you go down this winding path with us, it will sometimes hurt because it is so honest and real. But we're on this road together. And we're grateful you're accompanying us as we live the triune life. We want to be your Sherpas as you learn to flex your CQ muscles.

Remember our friend George Washington, who took a trip through all thirteen states, staying in the spaces and places of the common people? He was tracking and trailing his context, knowing it from the inside out.

Tracking has been called the oldest continuous traditional knowledge practice of humans. As any tracker will tell you, the tracks of an animal are more accurate and telling than the physical animal itself. Trackers learn to read indents on a landscape like literacy enables you to read words on a page. Trackers can read the sand like we read a road map.

Tracking has been called the oldest continuous traditional knowledge practice of humans.

Or like your dog reads you. Most animals, not just dogs, are natural trackers. For example, there are only a few dozen Sumatran rhino left in the wild, spread over four disconnected geographic areas. There are at most only one hundred in captivity. Called "the last living relic of the Miocene era," it emanates a sound that is as melodic as a singing whale or a whistling dolphin. The Sumatran rhino is calm and docile in its keeper's pen because it associates these enclosures with human habitats. But put the rhino in the wild and it becomes fiercely protective of its territory. It can read context better than some humans. And it sings when it wants to be fed or let out of its pen or be with its mother.[133]

Dogs out-master their masters at people semiotics. They are particularly good at reading their context and knowing by the body language of their human companions what we are going to do before we do it.

Robinson Crusoe discovered a footprint in the sands of a beach on a deserted island. He didn't stop to wonder if the waves had by chance washed the sands into an unusual shape. He instantly knew he wasn't alone. The same principle applies everywhere in the universe: If you find tracks, something caused them and put them there. "Whenever we discover some detailed structure, pattern or correspondence in the world, we know intuitively that a story of causes lies behind it."[134] But to see the details, you need to slow down, even crawl at times. If you take an express tour, as anyone can tell you, details fly past the window in a blur.

The Bible has often been compared to a road map, but a map will not do you any good unless you know where you are at. You need signs to tell you where you are. Absalom, the son of David, got hanged because he didn't know how to read the lay of the land. He didn't know where he was. It wasn't the first failure of contextual intelligence in the Bible, and there are many stories of low CQ throughout the Scriptures.

> *Today's newspaper wraps tomorrow's fish.*
> *—old saying*

For a high CQ today, we must separate truth tracking from trend tracking. Every epoch, every context, has its trends and trajectories. Which trends tend toward truth, and which trends tend toward evil and falsehood? We must also learn to hack our way through the jungle and jumble of three levels of culture:

1. high culture
2. pop culture
3. folk culture[135]

Each culture, whether high, pop, or folk, has its own thematics, semantics, and semiotics. Each level of culture has its own stored stories, shared stories, customs and clichés, alternative narratives, and hidden values. The details, decorations, and silences tell as much of the story as the speech and sounds. Each level of culture also has a rich variety of oral culture, with its own storytellers, comics, and embarrassment of blessings, curses, proverbs, puns, folk wisdom, and children's rhymes. It is not just high culture that boasts the professional argots of doctors, engineers, lawyers, and academics. There is a professional *patois* to be learned and respected in pop and folk culture as well, as evidenced in the world of chefs, wedding planners, and musicians.

Wherever you plant your feet, whether in high, pop, or folk culture, that space constantly changes. Do the harmonics of the Spirit start to rumble and resonate? Or do the vibes roil discord? Feeling the vibes is the open sesame of tracking.

Soft Eyes

> *"The eye is the lamp of the body. So, if your eye is healthy, your whole body will be full of light; but if your eye is unhealthy, your whole body will be full of darkness. If then the light in you is darkness, how great is the darkness!"*
>
> —*Matthew 6:22–23*

Tracking requires a different kind of seeing. How we see is important, as Jesus reiterated on more than one occasion. What does it mean to see the world through eyes full of light?

Tracking requires having soft eyes, which is a primary core competency of CQ. Alan Hirsch says having soft eyes is essential to hunters, detectives, and to all new discoveries and learning.[136] Think of Jesus's repeated conflict with the religious leaders. He often talked about their eye condition. He called them "blind guides" (Matt. 15:14; 23:16, 24). Their eye condition was connected to their heart condition, as they had "hardness of heart" (Mark 3:5; 10:5). In each of these encounters, Jesus highlights their diminished way of seeing others, their fixed views, and their stubborn resistance to take on the posture of a learner.

Their rigid, hard-eyed, surety of knowing leads them to accuse Jesus of hanging out with sketchy, unclean people and to dismiss his miracles as fraudulent. In response, Jesus says, "No one sews a piece of unshrunk cloth on an old cloak, for the patch pulls away from the cloak, and a worse tear is made. Neither is new wine put into old wineskins; otherwise, the skins burst, and the wine is spilled, and the skins are destroyed; but new wine is put into fresh wineskins, and so both are preserved" (Matt. 9:16–17). Perhaps the already hardened and stretched wineskin is the rigidity of the Pharisees' thinking. Learning from Jesus, the "new wine" would burst their minds.

Soft eyes are about seeing the world through the eyes of a learner. A world full of mystery, beauty, and unending adventures of discovery.

Other scholars have framed this skill differently. Paul Ricoeur talks about a *secondary naivete*. Walter Ong talks about a *secondary orality*. Whatever words you use, soft eyes is a skill possessed by horseback riders, athletes, learners, racecar drivers, parents, and lovers. Soft eyes enable you to see the hidden things in any context.

> *We are different people when we read a book a second time—and we are often reading a different book.*
>
> *—Indian entrepreneur Bharat Tandon*

Look around you right now. Wherever you are reading this book, stop for a moment and take a look. What is it you see? Describe your space. What are the first things your eye picks up on? With what emotions are you viewing your space? Do you feel guilty for not having picked up some clothes scattered in the room or for not vacuuming all the dog hair from the corners of the room? Who do you often notice? Who do you never notice? What makes you notice or not notice others?

What if one of us were to walk in your room right now and surprise you. How would you see us? How would you react to our sudden intrusion into your space without notice or preparation? What is the first thing about us you would notice or see? How would you size up your intruders, even if they were your authors?

Having soft eyes is often contrasted with hard eyes. Did you look at your space and your surprise visitors with hard eyes or soft eyes?

Hard eyes are fixed, firm, and confident about the context up ahead. Hard eyes have walked down this road before, a thousand times. Hard eyes are fixated on a goal or a destination, with a predetermined outcome in the cross-hairs. Locked in on the tree, hard eyes can be blind to the forest. Hard eyes are good for focused tasks that require careful analysis of a single phenomenon. The Western mindset trains the uninitiated to see the world through hard eyes—to analyze, deconstruct, critique, reduce to the smallest parts, then reassemble.

Soft eyes take the wide view, embrace the peripheral, and perceive as much of the whole scene as possible. CQ requires us to widen the lens and step back and look at the bigger, broader picture.[137] Horseback riders who have hard eyes get clipped by branches they never see coming. When we are tracking, we need soft eyes. Tracking is not about tunnel vision; it's about taking in all the details and viewing the whole context with the eyes of a learner. The best trackers leave behind hard-eyed assumptions and enlist all the senses to truly see a context, to look across the whole forest before focusing on specific trees.

"Do not worry about your life, what you will eat or what you will drink, or about your body, what you will wear. Is not life more than food, and the body more than clothing? Look at the birds of the air; they neither sow nor reap nor gather into barns, and yet your heavenly Father feeds them. Are you not of more value than they? And can any of you by worrying add a single hour to your span of life? And why do you worry about clothing? Consider the lilies of the field, how they grow; they neither toil nor spin, yet I tell you, even Solomon in all his glory was not clothed like one of these."

—Matthew 6:25–29

Jesus taught his disciples to see with soft eyes and warned of the tunnel vision that comes in a locked-in, hard-eyed pursuit of the satisfactions of material possessions. To paraphrase, Jesus is saying: "You trouble yourselves with worry as you barrel though life, pursuing superficialities. Stop. Pay attention. Look. Consider. Behold. Notice." These were some of Jesus's favorite words.

Look at the world around you with soft eyes. Loosen your grip and control. Don't force things into your own prehension of how reality ought to go. Move from an active and dominant mode of comprehension to a receptive and open one. Alter the angle just a bit, and a whole new world appears.

Be trackers of the Spirit. Open your eyes to see God at work in all the details of your life. Behold the world with light-filled soft eyes. Once your eyes get habituated to something, you have trouble seeing it. If you aren't accustomed to an environment, you see more of what is there than when you're accustomed to everything. Become like a child, wide-eyed to the wonder of it all. Let your senses bathe in the beauty, truth, and goodness of your place and space. Experience your context in new ways that take in the whole before you pick apart and critique the component parts.

Tracking also requires community. Every context has a *scenius*, which is shorthand for the "genius of the scene." Visual artist and musical theorist Brian Eno originally coined this term to refer to "the intuition of a whole cultural scene." *Scenius* is "the communal form of the concept of the genius."[138] This is why the cultivation of contextual intelligence is less the effort of a heroic solo leader and more the work of a community.

Hence our suggestion that you create a CQ team. It takes a team of trackers to see a context with soft eyes. *Scenius* is about "the ability, intuition, and creative intelligence of a community, group, society, or organization to create what they aspire."[139] It's a collective form of intelligence, occurring when a group of people sync their minds in an effort to understand a context and empower each other to seek reconciliation of the gaps within it. Observation without conversation issues in a deprivation of innovation and motivation for conservation.

Most of our schooling has taught us to see life through solo and silo hard eyes. Alasdair MacIntyre's *After Virtue* (1981) was an early warning signal about the fragmentation of modern culture and the partitioning of human understanding into separate compartments without unity and purpose and with a built-in prejudice against comprehending the whole, which is the goal of the human mind.[140] No wonder we read Scripture with an acute case of "versitis." We dissect numbered sentences, word by word, neglecting the wider scope and sweep of the story. When we tunnel vision into verses, we miss the particulars or dismiss the details of the story. But it's the details that tell the story. It is J. M. W. Turner's simple daub of red (a buoy) that brings the whole painting into focus.[141] Without Proust's "little patch of yellow wall" in Vermeer's *View of Delft*,[142] the whole painting or story or play collapses.

Il n'y a que les détails qui comptent. Only the details are really important.

—*ancient French proverb favorite of Mircea Eliade*[143]

We learn to view our contexts in this way as well. We come with hard-eyed assumptions about our community. Rather than tracking the context with soft eyes in fresh ways every day, we petri dish everything and put it under the microscope of a mind trained for dissection and deconstruction. We are wired to this method in a ruggedly individualistic way.

Tracking with hard eyes only allows us to see what we want to see. What we presuppose is already there. This is our fundamental fallacy, part of our miswiring and misfiring—to believe that the pursuit of something outside ourselves, even if it is "life, liberty, and the pursuit of happiness," is the greatest dream of our day.

Tracking is not about pursuing. It's about hearing into speech and sight, receiving into giving, and smelling into tasting and touching. In short, tracking is about deeper levels of community. It's about connecting the dots of the bigger picture and finding each other and the world in new and fresh ways. In tracking, the CQ team is careful not to speak before it first listens. "Speak, Lord, for your servant [CQ team] is listening" (1 Sam. 3:10).

Rev. Jill Beck (Michael's wife) and her team were tracking the Spirit when they accidentally created an interracial unity movement. Wildwood is a community with a history of racism, and the remnants of segregation exist still today. There is a railroad track through the center of the town with primarily black folks on one side, white on the other. The churches on both sides have been complicit in preserving that segregation.

Jill's team followed the Spirit across the tracks to build relationships. They organized a Prayer Walk for Racial Peace. Following the footsteps of the Spirit together, four hundred people sang their way down MLK Jr. Boulevard and stopped at an abandoned community center. Together they renovated that center and started a Saturday morning breakfast church for the kids in the neighborhood.

As they built relationships with these children through play, food, and Jesus stories, those caught in the illegal drug industry across the street befriended them. The team then followed the Spirit onto the street corner. They discovered their new friends had incredible God-given entrepreneurial impulses. Another kind of church was born as they dreamed together how they might turn their abilities into legitimate businesses. West Wildwood is a different community today. This team simply tracked the Spirit's trails through a sequence of relational interactions.

In tracking, get the lay of the land three ways:

1. tracking by sight

2. tracking by ear to the ground

3. tracking by nose (smell)

In Jesus's final teaching block to his disciples, he instructs them to maintain a state of watchfulness and calls them to "stay awake" or "be awoke" (Mark 13:37). The instructions are not "Wake up." The Greek word γρηγορω (grēgoreō) denotes a process of continuing. They were awakened to the love of God embodied in the person of Jesus of Nazareth and available now by the power of the Holy Spirit. Perhaps the church needs to recover from amnesia so that we can "stay awoke" again and not fall asleep at the wheel of Jesus's mission.

This ability to focus one's attention in order to observe and analyze the surroundings is one of the core competencies of contextual intelligence tracking and trailing. The ability not only to notice but to be sensitive to the larger, macro-level contextual changes to which these signs point is also a core competency. Jesus was teaching his disciples to "understand the times" and "know what to do."

CONTEXTUAL INTELLIGENCE FRAMEWORK
THE MIND OF CHRIST: Philippians 2:1-11; Ephesians 4:1-24

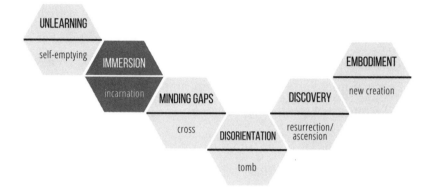

FYSA #4: *Solvitur Ambulando*—Context Walking

There is nothing like walking to get the feel of a country. A fine landscape is like a piece of music; it must be taken at the right tempo. Even a bicycle goes too fast.

—*Paul Scott Mowrer*

The Latin phrase *solvitur ambulando* means "to find a solution to a problem by walking around." A high CQ requires some serious *solvitur ambulando*.

According to legend, the Greek philosopher Diogenes was the first to coin the phrase *solvitur ambulando*. It happened like this. To stop a colleague who was in the midst of presenting a rational proof that motion was impossible, Diogenes simply stood up, walked away, and muttered in his wake, "*Solvitur ambulando.*"

Greek philosophers were some of the most famous walkers. Aristotle founded a school of philosophy called Peripatetics that linked walking with thinking. Greek seminars were not conducted with students seated, but teaching took place while walking and talking and debating. In Raphael's famous fresco *The School of Athens*, Aristotle and Plato are walking while discoursing and debating, their students consulting their textbooks and taking notes. Sophists wandered from town to town, lecturing to those hungry for new insights and ideas. The Stoic philosopher Seneca (4 BC–AD 65) admitted that his favorite metaphors for human existence came from ambling around Rome. Eventually, by the fourth or fifth century, walking and travel would be associated with wisdom since so many authors and sages did it.

Some more contemporary examples of context walkers include Charles Darwin, Steve Jobs (often!), and Cal Newport (Cal explains his practice in his book *Deep Work*).

Some scholars estimate that Jesus walked on average twenty miles (32 km) a day during his ministry, although he walked as much from table to table as from town to town. As he walked, Jesus taught his disciples how to hone contextual intelligence and read the signs. The imperatives of Christ came most often while walking, not standing.

- "Consider the lilies of the field" (Luke 12:27).

- "Listen and try to understand" (Matt. 15:10).

- "Keep watch; you don't know when your Lord is coming" (Matt. 24:42).

- "Look at the birds of the air" (Matt. 6:26).

- "See the fields. They are ripe for harvest" (John 4:35).

- "Move out to the deep water" (Luke 5:4).

- "Listen carefully. Pay attention" (Mark. 4:24; Luke 8:18).

- "When you enter a home . . ." (Matt. 10:12).

- "When you enter a city . . ." (Matt. 10:11).

- "Go and do the same" (Luke 10:37).

- "Have faith the size of a mustard seed" (Luke 17:6).

- "Careful. . . . Watch" (Luke 21:36).

- "Trust me" (John 14:12).

- "Get up . . . go" (Matt. 26:46; Mark 14:42).

To get the lay of the land, you need to go feet first. To bring yourself home, you need to walk your context. Think of your context of walking as a pilgrimage where you learn the geography of spirit in your place. Medieval maps weren't designed to get you from A to B physically (on land), but from A to B spiritually. They were visual statements of theological truth, which is why Jerusalem was always smack dab in the middle of everything. The geography you are charting with your pilgrim walks is as much a map of the landscape of spirit and mind as a map of the physical landscape.

Eight walks are a minimum.

First, walk it just to reintroduce yourself to what's there. This includes a day walk and a night walk. There is a night zip code that is entirely different from your day zip code. There is a world of light and a world of night. Different plants, smells, and creatures come out at night. Listen and learn your context both in its daylight and nightlife form. This means you will need to learn your bar culture, which can be the major competition to the church. William Blake put it like this in his "Garden of Love" poem:

And the gates of this Chapel were shut
And 'Thou shalt not' writ over the door.[144]

Or in his poem "The Little Vagabond" (1794), comparing those who attend church on Sunday morning and those who attend the alehouse

Saturday night:

Dear mother, dear mother, the church is cold

but the Ale-house is healthy and pleasant and warm.

While you're walking the nooks and crannies of your zip code, look for the good as well as the garbage—not just the discarded needles, syringes, and other sharps that increasingly litter the drains, gutters, and streets of our zip codes, but other hazards that require careful attention and disposition. Dwight D. Eisenhower called TV ads one of the sharpest "syringes of modern consumer capitalism, highly tuned and expensive products designed to inject specific aspirations and desires into our heads. It would be foolish to underestimate their influence over time."[145] Kenneth Clarke's landmark series *Civilization* (1969) was partly designed to encourage viewers to buy color televisions. What are the syringes of your zip code that are strewn everywhere but dangerous to pick up and, especially, to expose to our children? Some syringes are seemingly harmless but highly addictive, like ice cream.

Second, to assume a posture of placefulness, you need to walk your context to experience what's there with all your senses so that your knowing of your zip code is not just an intellectual knowing but an embodied knowing. Eat at every restaurant. Buy a little something at every store, and ask if the owner is present. Take a dog with you (borrow one if you don't have one), and let the dog scent some discoveries you might have missed.

Have a little fun with the churches in your zip code and see if the cliché of a "Saloon Spirituality" holds up:

- Reformed furnish the brandy

- Anglicans, the gin

- Presbyterians, the scotch

- Catholics, the wine

- Lutherans, the beer

- Eastern Orthodox, the vodka

- Methodists, the grape juice

- Baptists, the soda water

- Adventists, the Gatorade

- Mormons, the iced tea

Third, walk your context to savor its beauty and uniqueness but also its pains and fears. Walk in groups, and in the conversation in motion, see if your compass and compassion don't sharpen your imagination and make you more triumphantly creative.

Although not required, it is recommended to bring along a walking stick. The rod or staff or walking stick has a distinguished and mysterious pedigree in Scripture, beginning with the "rod of God" Moses was instructed to take with him from Jethro's fields of flocks, which struck the Rock, releasing water for the thirsty Hebrews; to Aaron's rod that first turned into a serpent, which swallowed the other serpents before Pharaoh and his minions and then turned into an almond branch.

The canes or sticks you bring on your walk can be metaphorical symbols of your various tasks in CQ gathering. Your cane can be a sign of the divining rod, the forked stick or striking stick that dowsers used to find water in the most difficult places. It symbolizes your mission to search for signs of the Water of Life in the familiar and forgotten places of your community. The rod can also be the symbol of your role as a stirring stick that can "trouble" the waters so that healing can take place. "My soul is troubled," Jesus said (John 12:27). Sometimes it's good to be troubled. Sometimes we are called to be a stirring stick to trouble the waters so that healing can happen, as took place in the two Jewish ritual baths known as the Pool of Bethesda and the

Pool of Siloam (John 5:2–9; John 9:1–11).

Sometimes your walking stick can also be just that: a walking stick that supports you on your journey and a handy device by which you can poke the holes—the dark corners and crevasses and caves—to stir things that are hiding out of fear and shame and abuse. A walking stick can help you find, before you fall in, the craters in a world cratered with loss and displacement.

Wade in the water

Wade in the water

Children wade, in the water

God's gonna trouble the water

Who's that young girl dressed in red

Wade in the water

Must be the children that Moses led

God's gonna trouble the water

Wade in the water, wade in the water children

Wade in the water,

God's gonna trouble the water

—Underground Railroad spiritual

Fourth, visit as many restrooms as possible in your zip code.

Hospitality is where guests are made to feel like they're the hosts, and hosts know what it is to feel like they're the guests. Hospitality is all about what it means to be a good host and a good guest. Being a good guest is as important as being a good host. And part of a high CQ is learning what it means to be a good guest in any context in which you find yourself.

Washrooms tell all—at least about a context and its hospitality. Just check out the graffiti in your local restroom or lack thereof. What is the writing on the wall? What does it tell you about the context? What is the condition of this space? Is it neglected, dirty, and missing the essentials of soap, hygiene products, and toilet paper? Or is there a personal butler with hand towels, newspapers, and mints? What does the washroom tell you?

Fifth, prayer walk your context. Faith needs footpaths of prayer.

A contextually intelligent person can not only walk and chew gum at the same time, but they can walk and pray at the same time. The prayer walk over your zip code can be done while praying, either out loud or in silence, either solo or in a small group. But the power of a prayer walk is first revealed in Joshua 6, where the Israelites prayer walk the walls of the city of Jericho. Their walk around the city became more a march on a mission, and with a loud shot and the blast of the shofars, the city was forever changed.

"Have you said your prayers?" As a child, my two brothers and I (Len) always expected those words if we were traveling. Urban Appalachians are always traveling, "heading for the hills" or staying in someone's house, which most likely did not have a tradition of daily family prayer. How many children at bedtime hear those words anymore, either from their parents, Christian or not, or anyone else? That question "Said your prayers?" is now associated with the last words victims hear before their brains are blown out by some villain or as a prelude to some other act of violence.

Before we make any decision about our context, decisions that may be brutal and bring axes down on people's lives, maybe it's time for us to ask each other the question, "Said your prayers?"

Sixth, walk to talk to the elders. The aged were given respect in ancient cultures because they carried the memory of the people. They were the historians of the tribe. Their collective experiences were protected like an armory of wisdom, a storehouse of treasures, valued like secret maps. We are a long way from this, but there is enough of a residue of this tradition still standing as to make the investment of time to be worthwhile.

Seventh, walk the talk. Walk Jesus wherever you go, a Jesus *habitus*. Jesus himself became the *Halachah*, the full body of conduct, beliefs, and practices that may be best translated not as "The Law," but "The Way to Go" or "The Way to Walk in the World." In fact, the *Halachah* in the plural means literally "gait" or "path." So, here is the distillation of the *Halachah*, which is found in following Jesus into the world:

- Dare to go out without two tunics.
- Dare to take risks for God without cushy 401ks and golden parachutes.
- Dare to offer the word and the work of Christ without a down payment.
- Dare to go in directions you do not wish to go with just some sandals and a staff—a way to get there and something to lean on.
- Dare to take "no baggage" with you. It's hard to take leaps of faith when you're carrying a ton of baggage.
- Dare to be a Jesus wherever you go.

District superintendent June Edwards released a movement of *solvitur ambulando*—context walking—on a massive scale. At her service of installation, she encouraged all eighty-seven churches of the North Central District (NCD) to get outside their church facilities and walk their communities. This is an area of North Central Florida that sprawls beyond Gainesville on the northern end and well south of The Villages on the southern end. The NCD includes portions of Marion, Alachua, Sumter, Lake Citrus, Hernando, Pasco, and Levy Counties.

June oversaw the organization of a district Fresh Expressions team, and they planned a district-wide event "From the Steeple to the Streets." These churches were encouraged to mobilize the average worship attendance of their congregations in order to visit identified locations in their communities and do three things: pray, observe, and encounter. And 13,628 Methodists went out to do some context walking. This has now been happening annually for the past four years. These Methodists are growing in their CQ, rediscovering their contexts, and planting new contextually appropriate Christian communities—over eighty of them, to be exact!

CONTEXTUAL INTELLIGENCE FRAMEWORK
THE MIND OF CHRIST: Philippians 2:1-11; Ephesians 4:1-24

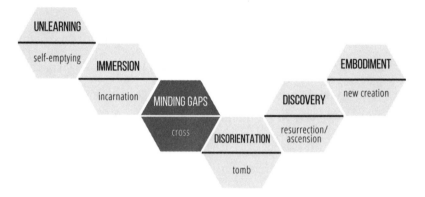

FYSA #5: In Touch, Not in Tune, with Context

A sure way of retaining the grace of heaven is to disregard outward appearances, and diligently to cultivate such things as foster amendment of life and fervour of soul, rather than to cultivate those qualities that seem most popular.

Thomas à Kempis, The Inner Life

In FYSAs 5 and 6, we move into "minding the gaps" in the contextual intelligence framework. As we immerse ourselves in the context, experiencing it in an incarnational way, we can start to make new obervations and ask new questions. A guiding principle here is to be *in touch* with the context but not nescesarily *in tune* with the context.

It used to be that Noah's Ark was the most famous boat in history. Now it is the *Titanic*. Noah's Ark saved people and the planet. The ship survived one of the worst disasters ever to hit the planet. The *Titanic* sank in one of the worst shipwrecks in history.

One of reasons the *Titanic* sank is that the captain and crew experienced a failure of contextual intelligence. They didn't properly read the signs. The Ship of Zion is facing a similar set of challenges. Indeed, in trying to make the church an ark culture, the ark is now a sinking ship.

The church's response to culture has been one of two positions. Either the church, afraid of culture, has tried to make church culture into a cultural apartheid, so afraid of being "of" the world that it refuses to be "in" it except in a bubble of borders and boundaries. The other posture, in an attempt to be "in" the world in a relevant way, is where the church copies the culture and everything the culture is doing, duplicating a Christian facsimile of it. The truth of the matter is that xerography is a form of xenophobia, the fear of not being able to compete with the culture or get ahead of the culture to a default despair of merely copying it.

In the meantime, Christians view each other with a hermeneutic of suspicion. That is, our first impulse is to doubt, question, and look with distrust upon others. We live in a deconstructionist culture, in which we are wired to take ideas—and each other—apart rather than taking an approach of "standing under." Seeking incarnational understanding of someone or something. Giving our withness. Listening to understand rather than listening to respond, critique, and deconstruct.

Jesus gave us a trinitarian equation for contextualization: *in* but not *of* but not *out of it*. His disciples are to be 1) *in* their context, 2) not *of* their context, 3) but not *out of* their context either.

1. *In* means that we need to enter the culture. Not sit by the pool with our toes in the water but get wet and dirty and immerse ourselves in the context. Jesus did not waterproof his disciples from the context of their day, nor does he expect us to do the same. Jesus's disciples don't mail it in. We go in.

2. *Not of* means we are to remember that content and context can never be married on this side of eternity. This is especially important to remember in a day when context is becoming content. Philosophy is being superseded or left behind by the semantics of contextual semiotics. *Not of* means we remain faithful and true to the content in whatever context we are in. *Prostitute* is a loaded word because it means someone of situational virtue. We all are situationally virtuous, depending on the context and who is present and accounted for. For a church universal always in mission and on the move, always learning to speak in multiple vernaculars and translate the faith into new cultural codes, exile is home. But every exile needs to be made a home. Hence *in* but *not of.*

3. *Not out of*—this third context part of the equation is especially prevalent in academic circles, where scholars love to be "out of it" in an intellectually "in" way. But we all need to beware of the "one oddness too many," of pressing something good too far, which is an ever-present danger and kiss of death. "I have so much more to tell you, but you can not bear it now," Jesus said.[157] Even Jesus was careful not to go too far or cross the one-oddness-too-many threshold. One of the hardest decisions for a high CQ disciple is discerning whether something you want to do or say is the red cherry on top of the sundae, that one thing which completes and perfects the creation, or whether it is the one-oddness-too-many that turns everyone off from what you are saying and doing and trying to accomplish.

One good way of summarizing this contextualization triangulation is to say we are called to be *in touch but not in tune* with culture.

The Greek philosopher Pythagoras (570–495 BC) called his disciples *akousmatists*, which translates literally as "listeners who stay tuned."[146] The precepts laid down by Pythagoras that his *akousmatists* were to follow were called *akousmata*. Maybe *akousmatists* is not a bad way to talk about disciples of Jesus, who are God's tuning fork to the eternal and God's perfect pitch. Jesus *akousmatists* seek to stay in tune with Christ, in touch with culture, but not in tune with culture.

Two of the most famous *akousmata* of Pythagoras call for contextuality: "Do not throw bread into a chamber pot" or "Don't cast pearls before pigs," a precept Jesus himself picked up and quoted (Matt. 7:6) as he explained in the Sermon on the Mount the importance of being context-appropriate, or acting according to the circumstance you are in.

> *What will survive of us will be quoted out of context.*
> —*English poet Wendy Cope*

Where's the Rub?

Every context has cons as well as pros, weaknesses as well as strengths. For example, some aboriginal languages (e.g., Tongan) have no word for *context*. You can't get more "con" about context than that.

The church is not encampments on embankments of flowing cultural rivers. But to be "in, not of, the water" means traveling salmon-style up streams rather than always going with the flow. Sometimes you will be alone against the pack. Other times you will be with the pack. But always you will be different from the pack. Or in Jesus's admonishment to his disciples, "What do you do more than others?" (Matt. 5:47).

If there is any need to remember that people with high CQs don't seek the approval of the howling hoards, the words themselves tell us. First, *mob* comes from *mobile*, which means always changing, always fickle, always volatile, always unfaithful. *Crowd* comes from the Latin *turba*, from which we get *disturbed* and *perturbed* and *turbulence*.

The gospel rubs against US culture in certain ways that is different than it rubbed against Hebrew culture or Greek culture or Roman culture.

The gospel is going to challenge different parts of each culture. We can respect each culture as well as see where the rub is with the gospel. The gospel rubs against US culture in certain ways that is different than it rubbed against Hebrew culture or Greek culture or Roman culture. We honor each culture in the ways that are consistent with the gospel, but we are always aware of the rub. This is the brilliance of the parables—the same stories rub in different places in different contexts.

Whenever you start feeling accepted, when you seem to be in demand, when it seems you're riding the crest of the wave and the wind is at your back—tack into the wind. When you're most at ease, you're most at sea. Or as Jesus put it, "Beware when all speak well of you" (Luke 6:26). The great are also the grating. When Bob Dylan was at the peak of his popularity, he went through a phase when he did everything he could to make himself unpopular. He announced his decision to retire from music; he got himself photographed on a pilgrimage to Jerusalem; he released a country and western album (*Nashville Skyline*). He did everything he could not to sink into the slough of stereotype and cliché and conformity.

People grow weary. We all know people who have grown weary in well doing. Logic is often for losers, and the best spinners become the winners. It's hard to be seen as the crank at the cocktail parties for always lifting up Christ ("Whenever you get Sweet/Beck, you always get Jesus"). It's hard when your friends run away from you after a sermon that calls people to repentance. It hurts for them to look at you and shake their heads and walk away. But our mission remains: *in* but not *of* but not *out of it.*

The mindset pervading the US church today can be captured by the word *ressentiment* (*resanteman*), a French word favored by Nietzsche. *Ressentiment* parallels the English concept of resentment but combines anger, envy, hate, rage, revenge as the motive of political action. It is a form of political psychology, grounded in a narrative of injury (victimhood, real or perceived) and injustice, based on a strong belief that oneself or one's group has been wronged. It embodies the sense of entitlement that a person/group holds, and it's expressed in a discourse of negation, the condemnation and denigration of enemies.

This *ressentiment* is fueled by a tribalism that takes the forms of primarily three theological cliques, which are in reality nothing more than the three major political theologies of imperialism. Here's a vastly oversimplified analysis, each position summarized by key words and the expression of *ressentiment*, that is, what it is pushing against:

- Conservative: Scripture and tradition; *ressentiment* against moral decline and virtue deficit

- Progressive: justice; *ressentiment* against inequality

- Neo-Anabaptist: alternative community; *ressentiment* against powers and principalities, state and capitalism.[161]

The existence of these camps creates an ecclesial ecosystem with certain tendencies. This is not an exhaustive list but highlights a few obvious ones:

- Eurotribal church structured after modern corporation assumes US social/political narrative

- Tribalism based in what you're against
- Allegiance to a tribe, sometimes over authentic faith and fruitful service
- Connectionalism by tribe, only in or out
- Elitism: advancement based on affiliation
- Hypocrisy: clergy and laity signing petitions even though they haven't actually busted a grape in the fruit fight for equality; waving banners for social justice causes while serving churches that are uniformly one race, one age, one party, or one sexual orientation
- Rewards for politically savvy and institutional guardians
- Destabilizers are minimized or exiled
- Skewed metrics that uphold the causal corporate logic of a perceived success
- Clergy competition rather than collaboration
- Looking for ways to discredit one another and discount others' ministries and churches
- Envy of success rather than mutual celebration of effectiveness
- Passive-aggressive ecclesiology
- The norm of niceness as a façade hiding intense disapproval
- Best practices of a minority of churches are showcased, which are largely irrelevant to the majority of churches
- Clergy too engaged in denominational hierarchy to serve their local church
- Distrust, decline, and exhaustion
- Innovations perceived and attacked as threatening or loose cannons
- People perceived as outliers of the major feuds and categories are

marginalized

Amid this dismal scenario, faithful contextualization should move in the opposite direction of social theory. The church should be a community that reflects the diverse singularity of the Trinity, not a reflection of the political camps of a current imperial iteration. One cannot have the mind of Christ and a will to power, elitism, and deep *ressentiment* toward a brother or sister.

- Traditionalists are right to value Scripture and tradition.

- Progressives are right to value justice and equality.

- Centrists are right to try and seek a third way between the two extremes.

- Neo-Anabaptists are right to be a faithful presence within.

- None of these positions embodies the whole truth, only pieces of the truth.

Our twenty-first-century context falls quickly into the delusion of relativism in which truth is reduced to what is true for me. Lesslie Newbigin quite clearly exposed this as a false facet of the ideology of pluralism and an "evasion of the serious business of living. It is the mark of a tragic loss of nerve in our contemporary culture. It is a preliminary symptom of death."[147]

It's also too easy for us to fall into the illusion of syncretism. One major casualty in this scenario is the uniqueness of Jesus or even a need for salvation. Not to mention the loss of the Scriptures as the primary source of Christian faith and theological exploration, containing all things necessary for salvation and authoritative for our lives and mission. This is the irreplaceable content of faithful contextualization.

Contextualization cannot discard content. A large part of discipleship is learning to bend our lives to the truth of Scripture. The Scriptures lead us not to an ideological truth but a person who is truth: Jesus, the way, the truth, the life. Jesus is the all-inclusive, all-encompassing love of God, contextualized for us to access and apply. He is the content for every context.

Being a follower of Jesus is not about running wild in our own desires, being faithful only to what is true for me. Yet simultaneously, it is not our place to convict and judge, only to love and embrace and nudge with grace and truth.

Further, discipleship is not something that happens only back at the church compound. We've often heard in our Fresh Expressions of church incredible life transformations. A young lady once said openly, "I slept with some guy Friday night and I don't even remember his name." As she sobbed and wept, the young women in that group surrounded her with a community of love and forgiveness, acknowledging the reality of her mistake while offering the gentle hope of a new kind of life. These stories happen frequently as we experiment with contextual forms of church where people live. They are safe places of communion, where new Christians can be honest and find healing.

Holiness is not about being set apart from the world. It's about pouring out the love of God in the places that need it most, like bleach that cleanses the contaminants of a context from the inside. It's about transfiguration that occurs fully within the world.

Jesus followers are not so much heard as smelled: "For we are to God the *pleasing aroma* of Christ among those who are being saved and those who are perishing" (2 Cor. 2:15). A Christianity so tuned into the culture you can't tell where one ends and one begins is not Christianity at all. That simply doesn't smell like Jesus to us. It doesn't pass the "smell" test. The content is designed to be in touch with the context but in tune with the Spirit.

CONTEXTUAL INTELLIGENCE FRAMEWORK
THE MIND OF CHRIST: Philippians 2:1-11; Ephesians 4:1-24

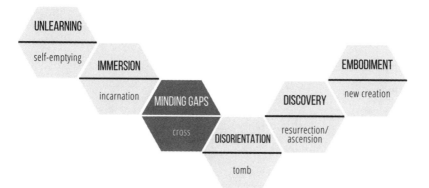

FYSA #6: Make Fault Lines Your Front Lines: Push Yourself to the Periphery

Anywhere I see suffering, that is where I want to be, doing what I can.

—Princess Diana

Jesus chose his disciples from among the outliers, the outlanders, from what we might call the Outer Hebrides of the Galilean scene. Jesus was a voice from the margins calling to the center.

Look for the most searing and tearing, the gutter and the skyline.

The power is in the periphery. Push yourself to the periphery. Be edgy—go to the edges, for that's where you smell the whiff of the future and see the formation of the new.

We're always drawn to the smallest room in the house. What's the smallest room in your church? The smallest house in your zip code? The smallest store on your Main Street? What is the mission of these smallest rooms, and how might you celebrate them better?

Jesus loves the "least likely to succeed category" and delights in giving them the greatest success. Where are the "least likely" categories in your postal code, and can you find stirrings of the Spirit in their midst?

"Low on the totem pole" is actually to pay the highest compliment. The low post on the totem pole is the most significant position since it must bear the weight of those above it—so it must be the most trusted and trustworthy and honored.

In a friendly neighborhood daily pickup basketball game, a random group of kids, a ball, and the local park are the only ingredients needed. On any given afternoon when critical mass is reached, whoever is hanging at the courts shooting hoops mobilizes into teams that play each other. Two team captains are selected; one gets to pick first, while the other team gets the ball. And yes, there is an unwritten code in the process of selecting your teammates: pick winners.

Usually, if you want to ensure victory, you begin by selecting the best players for your team first. As one by one, each player is selected, the handful of folks no one else wants on their team are left standing to the side. Sometimes those leftover players are placed on a team by default, and you do your best to make sure they never get the ball. Other times, if there is an overabundance of recruits, the ones no one else wanted head over to another court and play their own game.

No one really wants to be in that group, although they seem to have just as much fun. Have you ever noticed the way Jesus chose his team? In a world that, to quote Ricky Bobby in *Talladega Nights*, buys into the mentality "If you ain't first, you're last," Jesus shows a different way, one in which the least are the greatest and the last shall be first. Jesus seemingly didn't choose the best and the brightest for his world-transforming movement.

It's almost as if Jesus purposefully chose the leftovers—those ones no one else wanted or even saw. Normal, everyday folks like fishermen (Mark 1:17), then outcasts, untouchables, sinners, (Luke 15:1–2), even tax collectors (Matt. 9:9), and the formerly demonically possessed (Luke 8:2). It's like the pickup basketball teams of our childhood in reverse. Jesus starts with the losers. Nobody would have chosen these people for their dream team. No fantasy football picks here. This group isn't even Little League B-team quality! They were on the periphery, and Jesus chose them.

Jesus took people who knew how to fish and said, "I will show you how to fish for people." He took people's natural skill set and their circle of influence and trained them how to use those natural inclinations and abilities to expand the kingdom of God. He also patiently labored beside them as they failed forward and became the people he created them to be. We think Jesus can work with anybody, and we're living examples of that. In fact, he sometimes chooses the ones no one else would pick and uses them as agents of transfiguration within the context.

- Where are the craters? (In a world cratered with loss and displacement.)
- What's the dirt in the space where you are? ("Got any dirt?")
- Where are the "no go" zones—the danger zones? (There are always "no go" zones.)

"No go" zones: places where even the US military no longer sends troops, like Falluja and Ramadi, Tikrit, Mosul, Mahmudiya, large parts of Baghdad. These are places too dangerous for even the Marines.

Use the Micah 6:8 magnet. Pass the magnet of justice, pass the magnet of mercy, pass the magnet of memory over the jumbled iron fillings of culture.

Where are the fault lines? Where is the brokenness? Where are the cracks where people are falling through? How do we go about "netting" the fault lines—casting nets between the gaps of change?

One way to think about this in the contextual intelligence framework is *minding the gaps*, which originates from a visual-warning phrase issued to subway riders to be careful crossing the spatial gap between the train door and the station platform. For our purposes, this is seeing the fault lines, the disconnects in our community, the institutional voids where relational bridges need to be built.

For the church, cracks where people are falling through refer to the fragmentation in our relationship with God and others. Relationally speaking, there are gaps in our beings. A gap God has been seeking to heal since God first called out "Where are you?" in the garden of Eden (Gen. 3:9). There is a fundamental gap between the law of God, the covenantal relationship that God offers to Israel, and our ability to effectively embody the covenant. Jesus's own life, death, and resurrection fills the gap. Jesus builds a bridge. He is the net between the fault lines.

The ministry of reconciliation, this work of bridging gaps and netting fault lines, has been passed on to the church—indeed, it is our primary calling (2 Cor. 5:18). But when all the talk is on brokenness and woundedness and only faint fathomings of wellness and fitness, it is important to look for the rain splits and cracks that signify not distress and disorder but health and abundance.

When a tomato is ripe and rich in flavor and sweetness, just one drop of rain can cause a rain split, which doesn't signify a damaged fruit but a fruit overflowing with sugars and succulence. Church is not just an ER for the sick or field hospital for the wounded, but a health and wellness lab and fitness gym. Good contextual intelligence can detect when a crack is a sign of brokenness from within or wholeness seeping out. That's also why the saints hurt more deeply than anyone: the cracks of holiness.

It is not enough to leave Egypt; one must also enter the Promised Land.
—St. John Chrysostom

Through unlearning and immersion in our context, we practice mindfulness in a soft-eyed, "mind of Christ" kind of way. Thomas and Inkson identify cultural intelligence as a combination of knowledge, mindfulness, and cross-cultural skills. They speak of the danger of going into "cultural cruise control," in which we run our lives on the basis of built-in assumptions. In order to develop cultural intelligence, they suggest breaking out of this cruise control and developing an alternative state of mind called "mindfulness."[148]

Mindfulness is a very popular concept these days, perhaps so much so that some unlearning needs to take place to truly grasp its potential. Initially, *mindfulness* was a Buddhist term imported into the United States by psychologists and cognitive scientists who stripped the concept of its Buddhist philosophy. A mainstay of contemporary therapists and management gurus, *mindfulness* now means basically 1) slow down, 2) pay attention, 3) enter the moment nonjudgmentally, 4) receive the present, and 5) process the experience with a long fuse.

For followers of Jesus, our mindfulness also includes noticing the gaps in our context—gaps between truth and falsity, between racism and unity, between hunger and nutrition, between isolation and community, between sickness and health, between addiction and recovery, between consumerism and contentment, between commoditization and sharing, between extraction and trusteeship, between violence and peace, between worldly empires and the inbreaking kingdom of God. This list could go on *ad infinitum*.

Jesus does not send the disciples out and say simply, "Be mindful of your contexts." Jesus says, "Watch and pray." Listen up and pay attention. Enter your context and don't miss your moment. Then present yourself to those present and say,

"'Peace to this house!' And if anyone is there who shares in peace, your peace will rest on that person . . . cure the sick who are there, and say to them,

'The kingdom of God has come near to you.'"

—*Luke 10:5–9*

Heather Evans and her team at Grace Church in Cape Coral Florida went to the edge of their community and minded the gaps. They launched Eat, Pray, Love (EPL), a dinner church that meets in the Sun Coast Community Center, one of the largest trailer parks in the United States. Most people in this community were experiencing poverty and did not attend church, so EPL became their church.

Because many had no Christian vocabulary, Evans created a time of sharing "pows and wows." What were the hard things people were going through in life, the "pows"? What were the good things people saw God doing, the "wows"? This sharing created community, building relational scaffolding across the gaps. Not only did this team create community on the fault lines, but they recoded the good news in the indigenous language of the people. This is a team with contextual intelligence.

"Self-discovery comes when humans measure themselves against an obstacle," wrote Saint-Exupery in *Wind, Sand and Stars* (1939). Two of those obstacles need to be fear and the future. Because what are the images of the future? What are the fears? Because fears are real and fears activate all your senses. For those with CQ, the future is already here, it's just not evenly distributed, as sci-fi writer William Gibson might say. But futures form on the margins. The center is a fossil in disguise, a wolf in sheep's clothing. The periphery is the future, a sheep in wolf's clothing. Future in formation is found on the margins, not at the centers or citadels of culture. How to measure identification with the outliers, the outsiders, the vulnerable, the marginal, and the dispossessed? Go to the edges, the borderlines, the outskirts.

The call of Jesus is to be on the edge. Not stuck in status-quo centers but striking out in swampy wetlands and untidy peripheries. Disciples with high CQs will be edgy. They will reflexively go to the edge. But there are various edges to which we are called.

- Some will go to the bleeding edge. We call them martyrs.

- Some will go to the cutting edge. We call them mavericks.

- Some will go to the leading edge. We call them radicals and rebels.

- Some will go to the edge. We call them frontline entrepreneurs and creatives.

But there is no "What edge?" of feigned ignorance or selective blindness.

You will be accused of being "over the edge" or standing out there by yourself, "on the ledge." A few may find you cute, quaint, or the endearing side of eccentric. All will find you edgy. But without your edginess, there is no growth. There is one equation with four equals:

Growth = Change

Change = Loss

Loss = Pain

Pain = Growth

To increase your CQ, look for the liminars. The present conducts seminars. The future conducts liminars: liminal spaces of learning and conversation that have the freedom to imagine afresh the whole and explore the edges. "Ritual liminars," or "edgemen," as Victor Turner calls them in *The Ritual Process*, possess the radical potential of cultural transfiguration. "The essence of liminality," Turner explained in the 1970s, "is to be found in the release from normal constraints." Liminars have the power to "reveal the freedom, the indeterminacy underlying all culturally constructed worlds, the free play of mankind's cognitive and imaginative capacities."[149] The church can be such a liminar, but only if it moves to the edge.

The church can be one of the greatest obstacles to faith and one of the greatest incubators of faith. On a scale of one to ten, with ten being the highest incubator and one being the greatest obstacle, rate your church and its differing ministries.

Moses broke the Ten Commandments tablets when he saw people worshiping the golden calf. We break the Ten Commandments themselves in pursuit of the golden calf, bull markets, the golden goose, and Powerball jackpots. What are the idols in your context, and where are they being worshipped?

CONTEXTUAL INTELLIGENCE FRAMEWORK

THE MIND OF CHRIST: Philippians 2:1-11; Ephesians 4:1-24

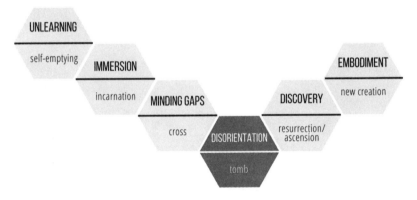

FYSA #7: Doing Time: The Discipline of Historical Context

Tradition is not a thing, it is an activity. To work within tradition is to make anew, not just to curate.

—*literary critic Seth Lerer*[150]

Before you go any further, check yourself. Have you applied the discipline of historical context? We have no right to decontextualize anything until first having contextualized it.

When your grandchild puts a skateboard in front of you, you have to exercise the discipline of chronological context, which is a form of historical context. In other words, you have to stop and tell yourself your age. You have to remind yourself of your demographic context. Because if you don't, it may cost you dearly in mind, body, and pocketbook.

Tradition is itself part content and part context. Every context is an environment, and environments need conservation and care and cultivation. Tradition needs conservation and care and cultivation. But contextuality is more than transplanting the old content into the new local, because the old content was itself partly context.

Tradition is not going backward, but tradition is not wanting to go forward without all the riches and resources available for the journey. To ignore the importance of tradition is to forget that Scripture and tradition leak and seep into one another in such a way as to make them almost one. In French theologian Pierre Grelot's phrase, tradition is the "source and environment of Scripture."[151] Tradition engendered the Scriptures before the Scriptures engendered tradition.

> *The great Christian revolutions come not by the discovery of something that was not known before. They happen when someone takes radically something that was already there.*
>
> —*theologian and ethicist H. Richard Niebuhr (1894–1962)*[152]

But tradition can be a vampire or a vanguard—a vampirish dead feeding on the living and a vanguardish dead feeding on the living. Tradition should not be undead but living. True tradition is not static but dynamic; tradition is continually being invented and reinvented. *Doing time* means not just curating the tradition but renewing the tradition.

Tradition itself is a creative act, an act of confirmed, consolidated, and adaptive creativity. But traditionalism is an act of calcified and fossilized creativity.

Traditionalism is when you believe it's important to stand by the ancient landmarks. Tradition is when you believe it's important to know where the ancient landmarks stand.

Traditionalism is one factor that diminishes the CQ of local congregations. When we become trapped in faulty mental models, we experience a form of "paradigm blindness." We think we are open minded and curious, but we are often largely unaware of how traditionalism shapes our perception.

We have heard the many stories of young "spiritual but not religious" explorers visiting church services, never to return because they describe them as a weird 1950s time capsule. When "we've never done it that way before" suffocates "maybe we should try this," it is often traditionalism that is the culprit. The joy of a living tradition is reimagining, reapplying, and remixing it afresh for each new generation. Living traditions must be interpreted and explained again and again so they don't become secret handshakes and members-only decoder rings.

British historian E. P. Thompson (1924–1993) warned about "the enormous condescension of posterity" that projects on the past its own superior position. We must learn to speak with the dead, to show our ancestors the courtesy of taking their beliefs seriously. Things were different in the past. We did things and thought things then that we would not do or think now.

Presentism is when we don't enter the past contextually, on the terms of the past, but by our supposed superiority in what we think and do today. The past is a context in and of itself, a different place that, like all contexts, must be judged on its own terms, without the present being imposed on it (presentism). We all live in bounded and locatable contexts. To judge someone from outside their context is to be arrogant, aloof, and, as Thompson noted, "condescending." The unholy alliance of nostalgic sentimentalism and presentism birth a yearning for a golden age that never was but to which we waste our time and money laboring to return.

> *The poetry of history lies in the quasi miraculous fact that once, on this earth, once on this familiar spot of ground, walked other men and women as actual as we are today, thinking their own thoughts, swayed by their own passions, but now all gone, one generation vanishing into another, gone as utterly as we ourselves shall shortly be gone like ghosts at cockcrow.*
> —*Cambridge historian G. M. Trevelyan (1876–1962)*[153]

Presentism is almost as bad as *myside bias*, egocentric reasoning that starts from a position of how this affects you or whether or not you like it. CQ requires the self-transcendence of anthropologists. "Writers can't function properly if they can't forget themselves," counsels British poet laureate Andrew Motion. You can't follow Jesus if you can't forget yourself, and you can't develop a strong CQ if you can't get outside yourself. You can't exercise contextual intelligence if you can't forget yourself. Or in more academic terms, the discipline of context requires the ability to embrace disjunctive reasoning and eschew cognitive miserliness.

There are hermeneutical chasms to be overcome, to be sure. The early church fathers operated out of an antiquated worldview very different from ours. Some of our ancestors hosted views on slavery and women that send chills up the spine. At the Last Supper, there were weapons at the table, which is almost inconceivable today. And as recently as the Plymouth community, every male over eighteen brought his firearm to church, and during worship sentinels paced outside the church. In previous cultures, before modernity, people had the script of their lives written for them by others. Now, at least in Western culture, we choose who gets to write the storyline and can create our own identity from scratch. Before history collapses the distance between ourselves and the people who came before us, the discipline of historical context forces us to come to grips with just how far that distance really is. The discipline of historical context is an openness to otherness in time as well as in place.

> *It may be incomprehensible to later ages that Brahms and Wagner thought that they were writing different kinds of music. But the fact that that is what they thought is historically important.*
>
> —*psychologist James Hillman (1926–2011)*

Every age is time-bound and time-warped. Every age gets some things wrong. Every person gets some things wrong. Every saint mentioned in the Hebrews "Great Cloud of Witnesses" got things wrong. You can't properly read the Scriptures without exercising this discipline of historical context. Even the most literalist Christian reads biblical texts as discourses not to be taken literally but rather in their context, within their time and community.

We have left behind selling our daughters into slavery (Ex. 21:7) or buying slaves from neighboring nations (Lev. 25:44), having no contact with a woman while she is having her menstrual cycle (Lev. 15:19–24), killing a neighbor who insists on working on the Sabbath (Ex. 35:2), not eating shellfish (Lev. 11:10), approaching the altar of God if there is a defect in our sight (Lev. 21:20), killing a man who has a haircut (Lev. 19:27), farming two crops at any one time (Lev. 19:19), stoning someone who curses or uses the Lord's name in vain (Lev. 24:10–16), and burning anyone to death who commits adultery with an in-law (Lev. 20:14).

Are any Christians actually cutting off hands or plucking out eyes that may cause them to sin (Matt. 5:29)? When is the last time you heard of someone who was put to death because they cursed their parents (Matt. 15:4–7)? When did we last destroy entire towns that do not receive the gospel (Luke 10:10–15)? Except for some Appalachian relatives, we are not wrangling snakes or scorpions or drinking poison to prove our faith (Mark 16:17–18).

There is no tradition in history that doesn't blush about its past. Even the high priests of today, doctors in their white coats, don't want to talk about some standard medical procedures in their professional pedigree. You don't think the medical establishment gets it wrong? Let's talk about hypnotoxins. Or what about phlogistons? Or ether? Or lobotomies? Or in earlier times, bleeding/leeching?

Tempora mutantur et nos, mutamur in illis. Times change, and we change with them.

Times change. And Christians change with them—at least, if we are to follow Jesus' in-time mandate to "do time" and to do time "on time."

Doing time.

Contextual intelligence requires a triangulation of three angles: hindsight, insight, foresight. We see into the future by having a depth of understanding in the past. We drive forward using as a rearview mirror God's question to Hagar in the wilderness: "Where have you come from, and where are you going?" Honing this skill of hindsight/insight/foresight triangulation allows us to do time, not let time do us. Matthew Kutz calls this 3D thinking.[154]

- **Hindsight:** Studying times past to chart a path for the future.

- **Insight:** Paying attention in the now, being in time and present.

- **Foresight:** Accessing the future through imagination and scenario thinking.

Hindsight.

Hegel warned that understanding always comes after the event and with hindsight: "the owl of Minerva (wisdom) spreads its wings only as dusk falls." The wisdom came too late for the dodo, moa, and great auk, and it can come too late for the Church too.

Insight.

Paying attention unites insights and outsights with intuitive knowledge and empirical knowledge to gain depth perception (that "third eye"). Insight brings together a bird's-eye view and a frog's-eye view to hologram a 3D view.

Foresight.

In history's march to the future, the foreseen is seldom seen. The unforeseen is. Wild cards and black swans lurk around every corner. When Jesus is present, anything can happen and probably will. Foresight is not projecting into the future from the past but prophesying forward. It is a feedback loop of the future calling out the past and pulling the present.

The transcontinental railroad—no one needed it at the time, many fought it, some mocked it, but everyone came to desire and depend on it. Same with the iPhone or what Steve Jobs dubbed in a prophetic label "The Jesus Phone." This is the problem with "find a need and fill it" and best practices.

Jeanne Liedtka, American strategist and professor of business administration at the Darden School of the University of Virginia, is particularly known for her work on strategic thinking, design thinking, and organic growth. Her article "Why Design Thinking Works" in the *Harvard Business Review* is helpful here. Liedtka describes the lack of understanding organizations often have regarding the way human biases (for example, rootedness in the status quo) or attachments to specific behavioral norms ("that's how we do things here") block the exercise of imagination and innovation. She describes design thinking as a social technology, a blend of tools and insight applied to a work process. Not only does design thinking help teams release innovation, it also "reshapes the experiences of the *innovators themselves* in profound ways."[155]

Liedtka explains how corporations typically rely on traditional customer research that has been collected through an impersonal exercise. Experts apply preexisting theories about customer preferences and review feedback from focus groups, surveys, and data on current behavior. They then draw inferences about customer needs. The problem with this approach is how it grounds people in the already articulated needs that the data reflects and how they see the data through the lens of their own biases. These methods do not uncover "the needs people have *not* expressed." Design thinking takes a different approach: immersion. This enables identifying the hidden needs by having the innovator live the customer's experience. Learning takes place deeply immersed within the perspective of the customer, co-creating with stakeholders, then designing and executing experiments.[156]

Immersion in user experiences can help us come to fresh and deeper insights about our community. In the contextual intelligence framework, coming back to the Issacharians, the first stage is reading the signs of the context, or understanding the times. This requires us to "do time" by taking this 3D angle.

One simple tool we have used with congregations to help cultivate this 3D seeing is called the "Remembering for the Future Timeline." Congregations get together with a roll of stick-up paper and colored markers. We draw a single line across the entirety of the wall and identify three major points on the timeline: the beginning, now, and the future. People then come forward to share significant memories they have in the life of the church: weddings, funerals, homecomings, outreaches, crusades, revivals, and so on. Once the timeline is pretty populated up until "now," folks come forward and share what dreams they have for the future of the church.[157]

This listening tool allows the congregation to share memories, hopes, and dreams for the future. It is an exercise in utilizing these three orientations in time: hindsight, insight, and foresight. Seeing the history of the church, and its reality now, establishes a sense of path dependency for what's coming in the future.

To excelerate your CQ, *carpe mañana* . . . seize tomorrow.[158]

CONTEXTUAL INTELLIGENCE FRAMEWORK
THE MIND OF CHRIST: Philippians 2:1-11; Ephesians 4:1-24

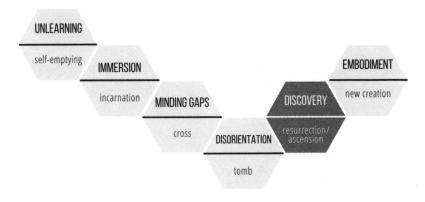

FYSA #8: Learn the Lens and Speak the Vernacular

Language is the road map of a culture. It tells you where its people come from and where they are going.

—*Rita Mae Brown*

Historians have taught us that our culture grinds the lens through which we view reality. Different locations have different cultural lenses that cause them to look at reality in differing ways. A disciple or community with a high CQ learns to take off their own *Kulturbrille*, as German anthropologist

Franz Boas, the father of modern anthropology, names the lenses that each of us wears and through which we perceive the world around us.

If you're still wondering about those *Kulturbrille* (a German compound word, meaning "culture glasses") that every one of us wears, consider the Western lens of "sex appeal" and how different it is from the culture glasses of other cultures. For women in some cultures to show their long hair, eyes, and necklines would be about the same as for Western women to show their bare bosoms. Flowing hair, legs, ankles, eyes, and lips are the highest forms of erotica for many Arabic men. To understand the hijab headscarves or niqab veil, you have to take off the Western lens and put on Arabic glasses. We take off our own *Kulturbrille* in order to put on the culture glasses that enable us to see a context as that context sees itself and learn from that culture.

Many of us still wear *Kulturbrille* that has a Christian lens. Very few contexts have a religious film, much less a Christian lens anymore. Is your context's *Kulturbrille* wearing a lens that is post-Christian, anti-Christian, pro-Christian, or remnant Christian (a culture cluttered with the discarded remnants of Christianity)?

Contextual intelligence requires the learning of the local dialect and speaking in the language of the people you are serving.

What does it say about a culture lens where the book *What Do Catholics Believe?* sits uneasily on the same shelf with a series that includes *What Do Druids Believe?* and *What Do Greens Believe?* and *What Do Extraterrestials Believe?*

What does it say about a culture lens where the History Channel features programs on ancient aliens, swamp people, MonsterQuest, and Project Blue Book?

Everyone speaks at least two languages. You are fluent in your native tongue, which itself has a variety of accents and dialects. But you also are fluent in a language you didn't know you spoke: images and metaphors. Contextual intelligence requires the learning of the local dialect and speaking in the language of the people you are serving. It requires both dialectical and metaphorical—the semiotics of the context.

This does not mean you give up your own unique vocabulary and vernacular or stop adding new words and phrases to your own. The cult of Apple has produced a bewildering vocabulary. Why can't we learn new words native to a new digital culture but not native to the history of the church?

A great example of the inculturation that comes from superior contextual intelligence on the ground is the Apostle Paul's famous speech standing at the Areopagus in Greece, which overlooks the Agora (Acts 17:16–34). Paul's CQ is off the charts as he uses cultural phenomenon as a medium of proclamation:

> *"Athenians, I see how extremely religious you are in every way. For as I went through the city and looked carefully at the objects of your worship, I found among them an altar with the inscription, 'To an unknown god.' What therefore you worship as unknown, this I proclaim to you. The God who made the world and everything in it is the Lord of heaven and earth and does not live in temples built by hands."*
>
> —*Acts 17:22–24*

In the breeze of these words, Paul may have felt the shadow of Athena's temple over his right shoulder. As he gazed over the Agora, his eyes recognized features of the equivalent of the village green, the public commons and marketplace of urban life in all of its aspects (athletic, artistic, economic, spiritual, and political). He knew his words would be competing with the greatest orators of his age, for the Athenian Agora was where the politicians and philosophers debated each other and showcased their rhetorical gifts. As he looked to his left, at the southwest corner of the Agora, he may have tried to spot the jail where Socrates was imprisoned. One wonders if Paul, as he began, thought of that great philosopher who was willing to die there to prove his innocence and model to the youth of the city the very thing he was found guilty of corrupting.

In Paul's day, the city of Athens was the historic cradle of Greek civilization. It had the feel of what we would today call a university town. It was a place that valued education, where there were two major schools of thought—the Stoics and the Epicureans.

The Stoics, a group of pantheistic materialists, followed the philosophical framework of their founder, Zeno. They believed that the various gods and goddesses did indeed exist but were vulgar expressions of primitive mythologies. They saw the universe itself as kind of living organism, the supreme god, if you will. They believed the pursuit of virtue was the greatest good to which one could dedicate one's life.

The Epicureans held to a materialistic worldview, first proposed by their founder, Epicurus. They also believed in the gods but were convinced they existed outside the space-time continuum and did not concern themselves in the affairs of mortals. They saw the universe as an arrangement of atoms governed by a series of natural laws. The greatest good to which one might devote one's self would be understanding these physical laws and living in harmony with them. Thus, as there was no value in an activity like prayer, for instance, this caused them to be labeled as atheists by their contemporaries.

The Areopagus (Hill of Ares, the Greek god of war) was in its genesis, the gathering place for the ruling council for the city of Athens. In Paul's day, it had become a forum for the exchange of free-flowing ideas between Epicureans, Stoics, and other philosophers. According to Luke, it was a place where people spent "their time in nothing but telling or hearing something new" (Acts 17:21). It was a place of dialogue and debate, where intellectuals could swap theories and disperse new ideas.

Did Paul challenge the church to separate from all this and be more agoraphobic? Or did Paul take his context seriously and say to those present: "See this monument to an unknown God? Well, I know him." No agoraphobia there. No culture phobia either. Only an eagerness to incarnate the gospel of Jesus with a profound contextual intelligence and skillful competencies in inculturation.

Paul recodes and reframes his message in the meaning system of the hearers by a process of *translation*, the ability to build a bridge of meaning between culture (context) and the gospel (content). But notice how Paul's Areopagus address starts constructing the bridge on their side of the shore:

> *Then Paul stood in front of the Areopagus and said, "Athenians, I see how extremely religious you are in every way. For as I went through the city and looked carefully at the objects of your worship . . ."—Acts 17:22–23*

Paul uses the inscriptions on their own temples to platform his proclamation. Temples to "unknown gods" expressed the deep religiosity of most Athenian citizens. In their minds, not to properly honor local deities could spell disaster, famine, and misfortune. These temples covered all the bases, so to speak. Amidst this pantheonic thinking of panoramic gods, mixed with the impersonal god of the Epicureans and the deterministic fatalism of the Stoics, Paul dares to weave his own introduction to a very known and personal God, the Creator of the universe.

He does this by quoting their own poets and philosophers: "for in him we live and move and have our being." This line originated with the native Athenian poet Epimenides around 600 BC. Stoic philosopher Aratus, who was also a resident of Athens, where he studied under Zeno himself (315–240 BC), wrote the tribute to "Zeus, for we are truly his offspring."[159] Paul does his homework, honors his hearers by using local voices, and shows his respect for their traditions by immersing himself in their context and worldview. Paul acknowledges the best in their culture and even nods a bit toward their pantheistic piety. But that is all a setting the stage for unabashedly lifting the truth of Jesus.

Paul also taps into impulses already present in both Epicurean and Stoic philosophies. He platforms some of their own ideas and acknowledges the crude nature of idol worship and primitive mythologies. Yet he uses their framework as scaffolding to build a compelling argument for the God of Israel, now revealed fully in Jesus through his resurrection from the dead. Yahweh is the one God, Creator of the universe, and the content of all. God is calling forth repentance and a turning toward true virtue. Paul invites all people to live a new life in harmony with natural laws.

Paul fully embraced the cultural reality of polytheism but used it as a medium for the proclamation of the uniqueness of Jesus. Acknowledgment of the truths within a culture primed the pump for drawing people to the Jesus well. In the West, we are all polytheists now. We serve many gods. Paul's both/and missional posture of radical openness and radical conviction shows the way for us to be the church in a new pantheon of god and a pantheistic or atheistic culture.

The religious and cultural ecosystem of the post-everything frontier is pregnant with profound opportunities for missional, relational, incarnational evangelism. The fields of a new pantheon and "posties" culture are ripe for the harvest.

The network neural society of the World Wide Web, a global integrated communication system, is the new Aeropagus. Spanish sociologist and Berkeley professor Manuel Castells notes that the culture of real virtuality

> *weakens considerably the symbolic power of traditional senders external to the system, transmitting through historically encoded social habits: religion, morality, authority, traditional values, political ideology . . . unless they recode themselves in the new system, where the power becomes multiplied by the electronic materialization of the spiritually transmitted habits.*[160]

Paul and his missionary teams were recoding themselves, reframing the truth of Jesus into the Roman system. John Wesley and the early Methodists recoded and reframed the Christian faith into the dawning Industrial Society, in "plain words for plain people" harnessing the emerging technologies. Recoding and reframing is a core competency of the contextual intelligence palette.

Castells calls it recoding. Crystal Downing, co-director of the Marion E. Wade Center and co-holder of the Marion E. Wade Chair in Christian Thought at Wheaton College, calls it re-signing. Cognitive scientist and psychoneurolinguistics philosopher George Lakoff calls it reframing. Whatever you name it, George Lakoff puts the importance of framing in no uncertain terms: "There is a basic truth about framing. If you accept the other guy's frame, you lose."[161]

Reframing, recoding, and re-signing is the use of Christian discourse to alter the context in which signs function. All our sacred images and idioms come out of a specific context where those words and phrases had specific meaning relative to their historical context. Over time, those meanings and nuances may have been lost or unhitched themselves from their original source, leaving us with the shell of images and idioms without power or punch. Re-signing (images primarily), recoding (words mostly) and reframing (stories chiefly) are the processes by which old metaphors and narratives are brought to new life to enhance effective evangelism and tell a better story. One re-signs and reframes and recodes by many means, coming up with new metaphors and stories and words that widen, narrow, or shift the frame so that the familiar can become fresh again.

To wield contextual intelligence is to wield considerable power. Why? The ultimate in power, as Lakoff and others have seen, is not position but the ability to set the frames and select the metaphors for the stories that need telling. We need to make sure we are wielding our power with proper motives. The Jesus way is not about trying to coerce, control, or manipulate people. Instead, we are meek with our power (strength under control). Therefore, CQ requires a team to constantly keep ourselves in check with each other and the Scriptures.

How, specifically, do you re-sign and reframe?

First, determine what the current framing/signing/coding is. Every frame/sign/code carries with it underlying assumptions that give that narrative power. We become proficient in the common currency of language, the stories, and the meaning associated with cultural symbols, then explore the pros and cons of the current frames and signage.

Second, use a new metaphor, narrative, or word that undercuts the status quo of the current frame's/sign's/word's assumptions. These new conceptualizations will redefine the problem and introduce fresh perspectives. The best reframing, re-signing, and recoding is done by revealing and highlighting hidden signs/stories/words hidden in the original frame but skipped over or suppressed by the dominant frame/signage.

Third, introduce reframing/re-signing/recoding action that features the dominant characters of the original location of the story. But do not take a course of action without injecting it with new memes and rituals, whether it be evangelism or faith formation or church planting.

For example, I (Michael) planted and pastor a church in a tattoo parlor. This is a semiotically rich environment. It is one micro-community of a vastly larger network. Tattoo culture carries with it a whole distinct currency of language, story, and symbolism. Artists even frequently use ancient Christian symbols (crosses, anchors, doves, fish, the Chi Rho, and so on), but many times the meaning behind them is lost. By being an incarnational presence in this community over time, we have learned the language. We use that sign/meaning system to have spiritual conversations about Jesus. Those conversations have evolved into a form of church meeting right there in the space.

There is no sermon per se, but rather a sermonic conversation as people in the group share their tattoo stories. As they explain why the meaning behind those symbols was so powerful they inscribed them permanently on their bodies, bridges of meaning are built and relationships are formed. We discuss a couple verses of Scripture, weaving those into the conversation, and then conclude with the Lord's Supper. New stories are formed, and old symbols are impregnated with new meaning.

While earlier examples have been found, stained-glass windows became popular in the tenth century as a feature of Gothic cathedrals. The windows were a so-called "poor man's Bible," created to illustrate scriptural stories for a largely illiterate population. The same concept was true of carvings, paintings, and mosaics. Every medium was used to communicate the signs of faith.

Just as these stained-glass windows told the story of Jesus to a largely preliterate world, emerging generations are telling the story of Jesus in their flesh to a largely biblically illiterate world. Using the available mediums of the day, they are reframing, recoding, and re-signing the Jesus story in accessible ways.

In an age where the space of flows and the space of places coexist and interconnect and a presence in the digital landscape makes a physical building unnecessary, contextually intelligent followers are harnessing social media and networking technologies to create Jesus communities in and among those larger networks. We saw this kind of Christian innovation on a massive scale during the COVID-19 pandemic quarantine. Christians "broke the internet" as they experimented with digital forms of church in lieu of face-to-face gatherings, many for the first time.

This accelerated groups of people connecting and meeting in communal spaces in new relational arrangements that looked like the church in Acts, recoding Christian truth into the system. We can be an incarnate presence on the digital frontier, harnessing these technologies that have become the means through which fresh expressions of church are organized, promoted, and sustained. We can supplement and enhance the traditional ways that churches once relied upon exclusively to engage their neighbors by creating "disruptive innovation departments" in local churches.

In social media flows, we connect with those outside typical church circles. Just as technology has become an extension of the human mind, so it is becoming an extension of human faith communities. Emerging generations who get their news through social media will also have their first encounters with churches through social media.

It is conjectured by Robert Paul Seesengood that it may have been illegal to preach a foreign deity in Athens, which would have thereby made Paul's sermon, which addresses five main issues, a combination of a "guest lecture" and a trial.

One irony of our time is that part of our context today is that the church itself may have become the Areopagus (the Area Rock, or what the Romans called Mars Hill). "Hey church: that monument you have built to your unknown God . . . know him." Or to put it another way, preaching to the choir may now be more difficult than, or at least as important as, preaching in the fields or arenas or streets of our world.

> *It's hell not to be in one's own time.*
>
> —*US/Canadian poet Robin Blaser (1925–2009)*

CONTEXTUAL INTELLIGENCE FRAMEWORK
THE MIND OF CHRIST: Philippians 2:1-11; Ephesians 4:1-24

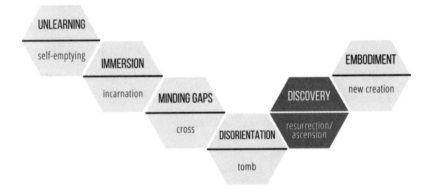

FYSA #9: Connect the Dots Until You Come Up with an Icon of Jesus

> *I believe in Christianity as I believe that the sun has risen: not only because I see it, but because by it I see everything else.*
>
> —*C. S. Lewis*

When the circuits are completed and the dots are connected, an image of Jesus's presence and power should appear in your context. The task of intelligence gathering is to see the future or, more accurately, to see the face of Jesus in the future.

We live in a world of three, not two, certainties: death, taxes, and data gathering. Issachar's secret calls the church to intelligence gathering, not information gathering. There is a difference. Information gathering is collecting and clustering data. Intelligence gathering is connecting the information dots and clusters. Most intelligence failures come not from lack of data or information but from inability to connect the dots of the information we already have.

This also requires us to connect the dots in our own mind, body, and soul. Data gathering is not a purely intellectual endeavor but requires emotional vulnerability. For the image of Jesus to appear in our context, we need the grace of the punctum in a studium world. There are two aspects of any image or context, according to French philosopher and semiotician Roland Barthes: *punctum* and *studium*.[162] Barthes's book *Camera Lucida* (1980) asks the question, "What makes a photograph stand out?" He answers with two Latin words: *studium* and *punctum*.

Studium is for Barthes "a kind of education (civility, politeness) that allows discovery of the operator." *Studium* is that which stimulates interest in a photographic image. It reveals the intention of the artist, but we experience this intention in reverse as receivers. An artist conceives an idea (or intention), then presents it photographically. The receiver then must act in the opposite way, to roll it back to grasp the ideas and intentions behind the image. You cannot participate in the image outside of *culturem*, which Barthes defines as "a contact arrived at between creators and consumers."

Put together two people from completely different cultures and get them to analyze the same photograph. Chances are you will get two very different interpretations, partly because of the different contextual frames by which we view life. Journalistic photographs were Barthes's prime examples of *studium*: "I glance through them, I don't recall them, no detail ever interrupts my reading; I am interested in them (as I am interested in the world). I do not love them."

Barthes calls the *studium* an "average effect," such as "application to a thing, taste for someone, a kind of general enthusiastic commitment, or course, but without special acuity." The *studium* is the element that creates interest in a photographic image, but is nonremarkable, drawing a "polite interest," the "very wide field of unconcerned desire, or various interest, of inconsequential taste."

What makes a photograph memorable is not the *studium* but the *punctum*. Barthes even speaks of the "grace of the *punctum*" in a photograph. *Punctum* is the accidental thing that "pricks you" and creates an unintended emotional response. *Punctum* is is the little piercing detail that changes the whole reading of the photograph, a metonymic power of expansion.[163]

In the global information age, we are wired to see, analyze, and communicate in *studium*. Contextual intelligence requires us to see the *punctum*, the details that prick the heart, daring us to traverse deeper into our own story.

You can't have *punctum* without *studium*. *Studium* is the canvas that releases the spark of the *punctum*. *Punctum* adds love and excitement to *studium*'s liking and interest. The *studium* of the context are the facts and features of the image. The *punctum* of the context are the magic and mystery, the awe and the wonder, that bring the *studium* to life.

Punctum is that aspect of an object or image that jumps out at the viewer within a photograph. The "grace of the *punctum*" not only pricks the heart but bruises the mind. *Punctum* exists alongside *studium* but disturbs it, defamiliarizes it, debriefs it with an element that rises from the scene but takes over the whole image. *Punctum* is the rare detail that attracts you to an image, and "its mere presence changes my reading, that I am looking at a new photograph, marked in my eyes with a higher value."[164]

In the church we are used to seeing and communicating in *studium*. Contextual intelligence is about seeing the *punctum* in the *studium*, the details that prick the soul, bruise the heart, and inspire us to delve deeper into our own story. It is this second element of *punctum* that changes the "like" of *studium*, such as the "like" of a city, to the "love" of that city, like the love Jesus had for the city of Jerusalem.

Punctum could be anything, something perhaps that reminds you of your childhood, gives off a sense of déjà vu, an object of sentimental value. *Punctum* is very personal and often different for everyone even in the same context. *Studium* is ultimately coded; *punctum* is not. *Studium* deconstructs the image, but *punctum* is the punch that imprints the image on the psyche.

What about your zip code bruises your spirit? When truly seeing your community, CQ involves noticing the *punctum* of your context, what breaks your heart, causing you to unravel emotionally. Connecting the dots is finding what pricks the heart of Jesus.

Local churches are the enculturated embodiment of Jesus in a particular context. Consider the massive variation of contextuality in the fresh expressions of a single church, Wildwood UMC:

- **Arts for Love.** Art enthusiasts gather to pray, worship, and create art together in the community center.

- **Blessing Bags.** A group worships and prays as members collect and distribute necessary items for people experiencing homelessness.

- **Burritos and Bibles.** Seekers gather in Moe's Southwest Grill for burritos, prayer, Scripture, and Holy Communion.

- **Church 3.1.** Young professionals run a 5k (3.1 miles), pray, and have a conversation about some verses from Scripture.

- **Connect.** A church for children involves fun activities, breakfast, Jesus stories, and worship in the local MLK Center.

- **Faithfully Fit.** Health enthusiasts meet in the park for prayer, devotions, and walking the track.

- **Higher Power Hour.** Spiritual seekers explore spiritual practices, including prayer and poetry.

- **Mascara Mondays.** A handful of women gather in the local coffee shop for prayer and Bible reflection.

- **Paws of Praise.** Dog lovers gather in the local dog park for prayer, worship, Scripture, and play.

- **Shear Love at Soul Salon.** A pop-up salon offers free haircuts, prayer, and a Bible reflection.

- **Skate. Pray. Repeat.** A group of friends gather at indoor rinks and outdoor tracks to skate, pray, and share their faith.

- **Tattoo Parlor Church.** Seekers receive faith-based tattoos and worship Christ with Holy Communion.

- **Trap Stars for Jesus.** Ex and current drug dealers learn how to start legitimate businesses, with prayer and Scripture mixed in.

Each of these new Christian communities is a result of connecting the dots of *studium* and *punctum* in a unique context. An interaction of culture and gospel, there is some gap, something that pricks the soul, that is being healed: boredom, isolation, hunger, lack of health, veiled beauty/artistry, or systemic oppression.

Imagine contextual intelligence as a grid that can be laid over any context to help reveal the hidden face of Christ:

1. Knowing self: How do your preconceived biases shape a context?

2. Knowing story: What is the God of our ancestors doing and what is Jesus already up to?

3. Knowing time: Using hindsight, insight, and foresight, what timescape are we in?

4. Knowing others: Who are these people and how can we be with them and love them?

5. Knowing place: What is this place, this postal code? Where did it come from, and where is it going?

6. Knowing language: What is the currency of language here? What needs to be translated, and what "tongue" is dominant?

John Wesley is a profound case study of CQ. He had to do some unlearning. We see this in his struggle with field preaching as a method to reach the pre-Christian people of the 1700s. Against the derision of his colleagues and all appropriate clergy conventions, he "submitted to be more vile" by preaching in the fields. After twenty years of field preaching, he wrote:

> *What marvel the devil does not love field preaching? Neither do I. I love a commodious room, a soft cushion, a handsome pulpit. But where is my zeal if I do not trample all these under foot in order to save one more soul?*[165]

Field preaching rode the energy of change from the emerging societal structure of the dawning industrial revolution. Wesley not only found ways to embody the church where the people were in his "world as parish" (the first, second, and third places of his day). He also adapted to the rhythms of their lives—for instance, the 5 a.m. gatherings with miners and farmers along the road as they went to work, which Wesley called "the glory of the Methodists."

While the larger church was targeting a smaller segment of already Christians, Wesley was targeting the masses of the uneducated working class. With the "plain words" of the gospel, he went to the miners' camps, debtors' prisons, and street corners where the people lived. He got out in the flows. He then manifested the church in their neighborhoods and networks, circumventing the bureaucracy of the attractional model.

Wesley discovered the CQ sweet spot, the Issachar mandorla of hermeneutics and semiotics.

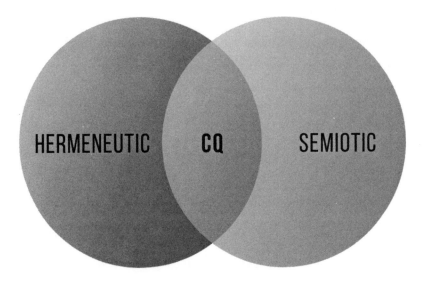

Figure 6: Issachar Mandorla

He suggested that itinerant preachers "search the Scriptures. . . . Fix some part of every day for private exercises. . . . Whether you like it or no, read and pray daily." For Wesley, daily engagement with Scripture was essential. Wesley also instructed his Methodist preachers, "Spend all the morning, or at least five hours in twenty-four, in reading the most useful books, and that regularly and constantly."[166] Study the story *and* study the times. Only then would they *know what to do.*

He was moved by the *punctum*, and he connected the dots of his context. When he did so, a beautiful portrait of Jesus emerged. Wesley knew Issachar's ancient secret. He read the signs of the times and knew what to do. Now you know the secret too.

CONTEXTUAL INTELLIGENCE FRAMEWORK

THE MIND OF CHRIST: Philippians 2:1-11; Ephesians 4:1-24

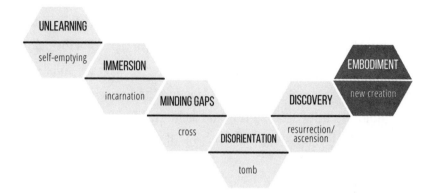

FYSA #10: Embodied by the Spirit

The Spirit liberates the Son from the bondage of history.

—Eastern Orthodox theologian and metropolitan John Zizioulas

The Bible is the worst how-to book in the world but the best why-me book, what-for book, and life-saving book in the world. The Holy Spirit applies the Scriptures to our hearts. The Living Word is contextualized in each one of us. One might say the application process is like the ultimate app.

Think about how the person of the Spirit takes a sermon, edits it, and applies it for each individual. There does, however, need to be an audit of the edit to make sure the Holy Braid (Scripture, Spirit, Jesus) has not been untied. A Jesus semiotics requires a Spirit hermeneutic. The Spirit teaches us not only how to read the signs but to apply what we've read and learned.

The body of Christ without the Holy Spirit is a merley a corpse. It is the missionary Spirit from which the life of the church is derived. The final move in the contextual intelligence framework is *embodiment*. When we take on the mind of Christ, it leads to a new you, a new social innovation, a new song, a new Christian community, and so on. It leads to the new Spirit-embodiedness of someone or something.

In an artist guild, the master artists have multiple apprentices working on projects together. The artists collaborated on different aspects of the painting. We think increasing the CQ in our churches requires a team of collaborative artists. The church should have less corporate office space and more artist/digital studios, learning laboratories, and atriums. More places of synergistic interactions where people create together on digital canvases.

The Holy Spirit is both a person and the life force flowing through these synergistic collaborations. Jesus, just prior to the ascension, laid out the missional plan:

> *"But you will receive power when the Holy Spirit has come upon you; and you will be my witnesses in Jerusalem, in all Judea and Samaria, and to the ends of the earth."*
>
> —*Acts 1:8*

That very pattern of the church's growth occurs throughout the book of Acts. Pentecost was a remix that enabled Jesus's instructions to develop. There is a clear parallel between the Tower of Babel, with God confusing the languages of humanity, and Pentecost, with God enabling the gospel to be proclaimed in all the native languages of the earth.

The wandering, wild God of the tabernacle showed up as the wild child of the Trinity, creating a new tabernacle out of a flesh-and-blood people called the church. The Holy Spirit enabled the disciples to go native, so the bystanders witnessed them speaking in all the native languages of the world (Acts 2:6). The Spirit didn't show up just to create a fireworks show but to thrust out the newly born church from the womb of Pentecost.

The power unleashed in Jesus's resurrection and poured out profusely on all nations at Pentecost—that is the kind of power that shapes us.

The Spirit becomes embodied in us individually and communally. The Spirit gives life to us, equips us, infills us, remakes us, and gifts us. The same Spirit that raised Jesus from the dead lives in us. The resurrected Jesus is an embodied, wound-bearing Lord, not a phantom. Resurrection is about re-embodiment.

The church is another incarnation of Jesus. Incarnation is the way the Spirit becomes embodied through us in our local communities. Embodiment is a primary way that God reaches out in love.

If we dare dream that God is very much in the resurrection business and is already involved in that work in our communities, then we can listen well to what God is doing and go join in it. We can be alongside our neighbor on the journey of life. In fact, we need our neighbors. We are not just there to offer them what we have; they also offer up something that we need. This is a mutual exchange of gifts.

Notice our focus is on healing, restoring, and redeeming local communities, not the local church. Also notice the goal is not to fix the community, take the community, or win the community. Healing, restoration, and redemption are a mutual exchange in the circle dance of the Trinity. When local churches understand the role we play in the larger ecosystem, as a kind of "green space" for communion, play, and fresh air, something amazing can happen. The community is transformed, new "churches" (i.e., communities) are formed, and many times the local congregation does experience revitalization.

Before we can ever be a witness, we need to be a withness.[167] Perichoresis describes the interpenetrating relationship of the three persons of the

Trinity, one to another, as the ultimate expression of withness. This mutual interpenetration, or the way the three persons of the Trinity relate to one another, reveals God as a community of being in which each person, although remaining One, remains distinct, penetrates, and is penetrated by the other. Further, perichoresis is used to understand the incarnation of Jesus as fully human-fully God, and because "believers experience union with Christ as a result of salvation provided by Christ, they also participate in the soteriological perichoresis with the triune God."[168]

The Triune God is a community of loving withness, Jesus draws the believer into this very community of being, and the Spirit indwells the believer. Thus, the church is the community of God's loving withness in the earth, in a circle dance that always makes room for more. The essence and form of the church is, in fact, derived from the life of the Trinity.

The perichoretic way of the Trinity is a shared leadership approach. Each person of the Triune God is an equal, not one ruling over the other. It is not the Abimelech (positional, hierarchical, individualist) approach but the Tola (shared, adaptive, relational) approach (Judg. 10:1–2). Most of the assumptions of the leadership cult flourishing in the church today are drawn more from a corporate business model than the life of God.

Issachar and Zebulun embody this shared leadership approach, allying together, pooling resources, and linking strengths and weaknesses. The entrepreneurial Zebuluns subsidized the scholar-practitioner Issacharians (Deut 33:18–19), while the Issacharians resourced the entire community with their ability to accurately diagnose a context and make correct decisions regarding what to do (1 Chron. 12:32).

Healthy church teams of first-class noticers employ this shared approach as they immerse themselves in their context. Rather than a professional minister or priest doing the work of ministry, embodiment follows Jesus's "priesthood of all believers" design. Mission on the front lines is about equipping a community of equals, the whole people of God, to operate in their Spirit-gifted abilities as apostles, prophets, evangelists, shepherds, and teachers (Eph. 4:11–12). Everyone who is a follower of Jesus is also a leader of others. We all have a part to play in the body of Christ (1 Cor. 12).

Many congregations have brilliant ideas that get stuck in the board room at the church compound. We are wired for causal logic, crafting a vision statement and then creating strategic goals: if we do A, B, and C, it will equal D. High CQ teams employ effectual reasoning; they start with the D, or the what and who they have right then, and iterate, experiment, and prototype new A, B, and Cs as they go along. As they make connections in the community, they form strategic partnerships with persons of peace (Luke 10:6)—people who unlock the relational networks in their community, who invite them to the table.

The Holy Spirit has been downloaded into our being in a very real way. It is how the Spirit of Jesus becomes the new and living wellspring of our lives. We have a new operating system and a new app for every possible context and situation. So, we are never without the necessary power and tools we need on any missional frontier.

If we accept that our real purpose is not to fix our community but to embrace the witness of be there with all, it completely alters our rhythms of being. Our entire understanding of service and mission is turned topsy-turvy. Overcoming isolation does not look to technology to solve the problem but rather sees it as a tool to create witness.

It is not our perceived power, our superior knowledge, our studied expertise, or our developed skill that enables us to fix and manage. In fact, these are the very things that may have gotten us into the very state we are in, a detriment more than a compliment. The church is not here to "claim this territory for the kingdom" or "take back our neighborhood" or "give back to the city." It's time to quit claiming and taking and discover the power of embodiment. We can find new ways to ask Eugene Peterson's pastor's question: "Who are these people, and how can I be with them in such a way that we can become what God is making us?"

The Holy Spirit is not focused on creating a "Christian culture." The Holy Spirit is focused on bringing Christ to life and being a transfiguring presence within every culture. If we ask who is our neighbor and ponder how can we be with them, we will stop looking at our community as disadvantaged and in need of our skills and resources and start looking at others in the same way God does, as people we just want to be with.

Instead of arms full of new strategies and corporate solutions, what if we just come empty-handed, ready to form relationship and love people? This will also help us steer clear of the proclivity to dump and run, to deliver our solutions and retreat to our walls. We will come less ready to talk and more prepared to listen. We can leave the tracts, Romans Road, and sinner's prayer behind and pray for relationships that bring healing and hope. Time with others is no longer a means to an end but the end itself. Relationships are the healing balm of life.

This does not mean that we will no longer engage in projects for our neighborhood. But the purpose of our projects has been infused with new meaning. In the process of alleviating hunger, healing the sick, and clothing the naked, we are forming relationships. Programs will come and go, but the genuine witness will remain. We don't need to engage in these endeavors because it is the sign of a healthy missional church or it gives us measurable statistics to report or because we are powerfully building God's kingdom (as if we could do that on God's behalf). These endeavors enable us to join God in being "in, with, and under" another as we expand the witness and usness of Emmanuel, God with us.

The people in our neighborhoods have what we need—themselves. Our community already has everything it needs to experience healing and redemption. If we overcome the obstacles of isolation and translation, the kingdom of God comes on earth as it is in heaven.

The Zechariah principle is easily amended: "Not by might, not by power, but by my Spirit, says the Lord" (Zech. 4:6). We remember the first two but forget the third: "Not by might, not by power . . . but it is by programs and plans and blueprints and systems and strategies and the latest in franchise church." No, it is by the Spirit's resurrection power, which is the power of creation itself, that is the primary resource of the church. The power of the Spirit is a power of wooing and cooing, a power that comes from self-denial and self-sacrifice, a power derived from service that flows from God's abundance. Spirit power is what overcomes isolation and desolation. Spirit power is characterized by love and fueled in forgiveness and friendship.[169]

Spirit power is missional, relational, incarnational power. The problem with this relational arrangement is that it defies the marketolatry of Wall Street that most churches have subconsciously adopted as their legitimating narrative. You can't whiteboard and flowchart withness or the Holy Spirit's power. You can't tweak programs to rain down the Spirit. You can't bring in a resurrection expert to consult with your congregation and form strategic goals for the next five years.

Contextual intelligence finds the solutions that are already present in the context, waiting to be discovered and uncovered. With the Holy Spirit as our Ultimate App, the church does not depend on outside research and outside consultants to solve its problems. It brings in outside research and outside consultants to uncover and refine the questions for the answers that are already lurking in its midst. You need coaches and consultants because finding the answers is easier than defining the questions.

Jackson Wu reports a major failure of contextual intelligence in a large suburban church he once served as youth pastor. The church brought in a consulting firm, through which they became aware of many East Asians living close to the church facility. A debate erupted on whether this church should minister to the "Orientals," as one church leader called them. They asked if these strangers would "be able to adjust to their tradition." [170]

They were stuck in a faulty mental model, unable to have the soft eyes to see from the perspective of their assumed other. Will the people we are trying to reach "be able to adapt to our tradition"? This is the wrong question, but unfortunately it is the death-rattle gasp of many congregations. Regarding the Gentiles, the Holy Spirit told Peter "to go with them and not to make a distinction between them and us" (Acts 11:12). The Spirit is always inviting us into a journey of unlearning, immersion, minding the gaps, disorientation, discovery, and embodiment as we seek to know, love, and serve the people in our context. We simply plant the seed of the gospel and let it grow wild in native ways.

The potential of a seed is lost if it's never planted. The content has to find a context. A tree is not the result of a seed; it's the result of a seed interacting with a context. A seed needs soil, water, nutrients, and fertilizer to become a tree. A tree is a result of a faithful relationship between content and context.

The Holy Spirit is always empowering us to plant the seeds of the gospel in new contextual soils. Churches spring up from relationships between content and context. We hope what we've offered will help enable you to grow in your CQ so that new people will come to know the person who is the content of that gospel, Jesus Christ.

CHAPTER 12

THE FINISHING TOUCH

"The Holy Hum"

The important thing is not to stop questioning. Curiosity has its
own reason for existing. One cannot help but be in awe when he
contemplates the mysteries of eternity, of life, of the marvelous
structure of reality. It is enough if one tries merely to comprehend a
little of this mystery every day. Never lose a holy curiosity.

—Albert Einstein

If you want a neat three points and a prayer or a happily ever after, you
won't find it here. As aggravating as that is to our Western mental model, we
offer rather a finishing touch. Master artists don't seek to conclude their work
by wrapping everything up with a neat little bow. Rather, they invoke in the
beholder a sense of unresolved mystery. So, we invite you to ponder the *holy
hum*, the universal that resonates through every particular.

Sharawaji is a mysterious word befitting a mysterious concept: the perfect
sound.[171] Nobody can agree on how to spell it (*sharawaggi, sharawadgi,*

sharawaji). No one agrees on whether it came from travelers returning from Japan or China. No one can agree on whether its derivation is from landscape architecture or the world of music. No one knows exactly what it means other than combinations of bless, bliss, beauty, and sound.[172] Sharawadji is a sonic state of heaven on earth, "an aesthetic effect that characterizes the feeling of plenitude that is sometimes created by the contemplation of a sound motif or a complex soundscape of inexplicable beauty."[173]

Philosopher, composer, and jazz musician David Rothenberg has built a whole book on this one word, *Sharawaji*. His triptych of books on the music of Noah's ark focuses on whale music, bird music, and bug music. After the triple exploration of the universal animal kingdom, he narrows his focus to one particular sound, the music of the nightingale, which he explores in film, in two-disc release, and in print. *Nightingales in Berlin* (2019) tells the story of searching the world for the "perfect sound," which Rothenberg calls the Sharawaji Effect.

> *The perfect sound is only made when there is total unity and harmony with one's context.*

The perfect sound is only made when there is total unity and harmony with one's context. A sonic ecosystem that is totally integrated with its time and place, a connection of content and context that becomes almost sacramental in its communion, is called the Sharawaji Effect.

We have written this book to share with you Issachar's secret in the hopes that the harmony of Word and flesh, Spirit and matter, story and song can be yours. "And I turned to see the voice" (Rev. 1:12). In the biblical drama, hearing becomes seeing, voice becomes vision, the ears open the eyes.

When a sailboat is maxed out in the wind, its sails unfurled in a total unity of wind, water, and weight, the boat actually lifts a bit and levitates out of the water. The sailor knows they have achieved that concord with their context when they hear a faint hum. Sailboat racers listen for the hum because, until you hear its sound, you can still go farther faster.

So, we leave you with the greatest of all of Issachar's secrets: the holy hum. It's the gift of the Creator of the cosmos if you connect content and context. You might also call it listening for the still, small voice (1 Kings 19:11–13).

ENDNOTES

1 Nathan Moskowitz, "Tola the Judge: A New Midrashic Analysis," Jewish Bible Quarterly 43, no. 1 (January 2015): 17, https://jbqnew.jewishbible.org/assets/Uploads/431/jbq_431_moskowitztola.pdf.

2 Nathan Moskowitz, "Tola the Judge: A New Midrashic Analysis," Jewish Bible Quarterly 43, no. 1 (January 2015): 17, https://jbqnew.jewishbible.org/assets/Uploads/431/jbq_431_moskowitztola.pdf.

3 Ibid., 18.

4 Ibid.

5 Ibid., 19.

6 Ibid.

7 Ibid.

8 Ibid.

9 Ibid.

10 Ibid.

11 Ibid.

12 See the work of Rosabeth Moss Kanter.

13 Moskowitz, 19.

14 Ibid.

15 Ibid., 20.

16 Albert Manguel, *A History of Reading*, the epigraph to Chris Arthur's Reading Life (2017); T. K. Das, *The Subjective Side of Strategy Making: Future Orientations and Perceptions of Executives* (New York: Praeger, 1986), 19.

17 Patrick T. Terenzini, "On the Nature of Institutional Research and the Knowledge and Skills It Requires," Research in Higher Education 34, no. 1 (1993): 1–10.

18 Terenzini, 1993, 6.

19 Matthew R. Kutz, *Contextual Intelligence: Smart Leadership for a Constantly Changing World* (Perrysburg, OH: RTG Publishing, 2013), 8–9.

20 Vincent J. Donovan, *Christianity Rediscovered* (Maryknoll, NY: Orbis Books, 2003), 25.

21 Kutz, *Contextual Intelligence*, 68.

22 T. H. Breen, *George Washington's Journey: The President Forges a New Nation* (New York: Simon and Schuster, 2016).

23 For more, see Leonard Sweet, *Rings of Fire* (2019), Joseph Tainter, *The Collapse of Complex Societies* (1990), and Nassim Nicholas Taleb, T*he Black Swan: The Impact of the Highly Improbable* (2007).

24 See Leonard Sweet, *Faithquakes* (1994), *SoulTsunami* (1999), *AquaChurch* (1999), *Postmodern Pilgrims* (2000), *Carpe Manana* (2001), *The Church of the Perfect Storm* (2010), *Viral* (2012), etc.

25 Their research was published in the book *In Their Time: The Greatest Business Leaders of the Twentieth Century* (2005). They collected and then computerized extensive profiles of these leaders and divided them into three basic leadership archetypes: leaders, managers, and entrepreneurs.

26 Ibid.

27 Max H. Bazerman, "Becoming a First-Class Noticer," Harvard Business Review (July–August 2014), and his subsequent book, *The Power of Noticing: What the Best Leaders See* (New York: on and Schuster, 2015).

28 Tarun Khanna, "Contextual Intelligence," Harvard Business Review 92, no. 9 (September 2014): 58–68.

29 MIT's Peter M. Senge is famous for his five disciplines of a learning organization, one of which is mental models, which he defines as "deeply held internal images of how the world works, images that limit us to familiar ways of thinking and acting." Senge also asserts, "We are not consciously aware of our mental models or the effects they have on our behavior." *The Fifth Discipline: The Art and Practice of the Learning Organization* (2006).

30 Khanna coins this phrase in his book with Krishna G. Palepu, *Winning in Emerging Markets: A Road Map for Strategy and Execution* (HBRPress, 2010).

31 TC Choong, *The Kingdom of God and Jesus' Contextual Intelligence* (Singapore: Armour Publishing, 2017), 15, 11.

32 Jenny Odell, *How to Do Nothing: Resisting the Attention Economy* (Brooklyn: Melville House, 2019), xxi.

33 Michael Polanyi, *The Tacit Dimension* (New York: Anchor Books, 1967), 24–25.

34 As quoted in J. Oswald Sanders, *Spiritual Leadership: Principles of Excellence for Every Believer*, updated ed. (Chicago: Moody Publishers, 2007), 56.

35 View online and learn more about PJ Crook at http://www.pjcrook.com/altarpiece.html

36 This piece is widely accessible online and can also be found at https://en.wikipedia.org/wiki/ The_Last_Supper_(Leonardo)#/media/File:The_Last_Supper_-_Leonardo_Da_Vinci_-_High_Resolution_32x16.jpg.

37 For the full back story, see Ross King's very insightful *Leonardo and The Last Supper* (Bloomsbury, 2012).

38 "'Contextual intelligence' means you have the ability to see from another's eyes, to hear the unfamiliar, to learn the strange, to understand in a different way." Leonard Sweet, *So Beautiful: God's Design for Life and the Church* (Colorado Springs, CO: David C. Cook, 2009), 201.

39 Odell, xvii.

40 Sr. Mary David, *The Joy of God: Collected Writings* (Bloomsbury, 2019).

41 Even the best historians (not to mention theologians) often miss this. For example, British historian Felipe Fernández-Armesto has suggested that a "third way" alternative to the economic cultures of communism and capitalism might be Christianity. See his excellent *Out of Our Minds: What We Think and How We Came to Think It* (2019).

42 These thoughts are inspired by Rupert Shortt's echoing of Terry Eagleton that "God remakes human nature from within by defenseless love, rather than by producing a banner in the heavens inscribed 'I'M HERE YOU IDIOTS,' as Terry Eagleton has wryly accused the New Atheists of demanding." For more see "A Slave in Your Place: What Does It Mean to Claim That Jesus Died for the Sins of the World?" Times Literary Supplement, 30 March 2018, 42–43.

43 Jackson Wu, *One Gospel for all Nations: A Practical Approach to Biblical Contextualization* (2015), xxii.

44 *The Shattering of Loneliness* (2018).

45 From the hymn of Samuel Stennett, "On Jordan's Stormy Banks I Stand," *The United Methodist Hymnal: Book of United Methodist Worship* (Nashville: The United Methodist Publishing House, 1989), 724.

46 Ibid.

47 For an exploration of H. Richard Niebuhr's classic *Christ and Culture*, see Len's introduction in Leonard I. Sweet and Andy Crouch, *The Church in Emerging Culture: Five Perspectives (El Cajon, CA: Youth Specialties*, 2003).

48 This world is not a conclusion; A sequel stands beyond, Invisible, as music,

But positive, as sound.

It beckons and it baffles;

Philosophies don't know,

And through a riddle, at the last, Sagacity must go.

To guess, it puzzles scholars; To gain it, men have shown Contempt of generations, And crucifixion known.

From "Part Four: Time and Eternity"

49 Watch a brief but fascinating segment on the fragility of whales, how they breathe, trophic cascades, and how they transform the climate at https://youtu.be/4Ei2yQY7DWE.

50 "Blessed be the God and Father of our Lord Jesus Christ, who hath blessed us with all spiritual blessings in heavenly places in Christ" (Eph. 1:3). He uses this a total of five times in Ephesians, including 1:20; 2:6; 3:10; 6:12.

51 Odell, 154.

52 Remi Brague, *Curing Mad Truths: Medieval Wisdom for the Modern Age* (Notre Dame Press, 2019), 89.

53 "Responses to the Lineamenta," East Asian Pastoral Review (Manila) 35, no. 1 (1998), 75.

54 Soren Kierkegaard, *Either/Or* (1843), 1:101.

55 Time Magazine, May 1, 1966.

56 As quoted by Joanna Adams, September 23, 2001, Trinity Presbyterian Church, Atlanta, and referenced by John M. Buchanan, "The Toughest Commandment," November 4, 2001.

57 See, in order of named examples, John 9:2–3; Mark 3:1–6; Luke 8:42–48.

58 Biblical scholar Ben Witherington is the first person we know of to call it thus.

59 Sister Mary David, *The Joy of God*.

60 See https://youtu.be/6Af6b_wyiwI.

61 Kevin Loria, "Bill Gates thinks a coming disease could kill 30 million people within 6 months

—and says we should prepare for it as we do for war," Business Insider, April 27, 2018, https:// www.businessinsider.com/bill-gates-warns-the-next-pandemic-disease-is-coming-2018-4.

62 Quoted in obituary for "Ann Nelson" by Dylan Loeb McClain, The New York Times, August 26, 2019, https://www.nytimes.com/2019/08/26/science/ann-nelson-dies.html.

63 The best treatment of the concept of recoding comes from Manuel Castells.

64 The best treatment of the concept of reframing comes from George Lakoff.

65 See *Sweet, So Beautiful*.

66 Augustine, *On Christian Teaching*, trans. R. P. H. Green (Oxford: Oxford University Press, 1997), 1.29.29.

67 Putting people in holes is the Enneagram or psychological assessments like the Myers-Briggs, which two million people take a year. Two million people a year take this assessment test, which has been called "astrology for middle management," or what Foucault would call "technologies of the self."

68 Joe Queenan, "The Case for Staying Put," The Rotarian, April 2011, 44ff.

69 See Quassim Cassam, *Vices of the Mind: From the Intellectual to the Political* (Oxford: Oxford University Press, 2019).

70 This story is told by Wade Davis, "Forests of the Milk River," Wild Earth 3 (1994).

71 By Starquake, we don't mean the title of a novel or the name of a video game. We mean the explosion of energy that astrophysicists talk about when they project what happens when the densest structure in the universe, a neutron star, suddenly is smashed open.

72 From an interview with a journalist from *The New York Times*, 12 March 1944; *The Expanded Quotable Einstein*, collected and edited by Alice Calaprice (Princeton University Press, 2000), 14.

73 Standardized tests like Stanford-Binet and Wechsler Adult Intelligence Scale (WAIS) or Wechsler Intelligence Scale for Children (WISC).

74 Cross-cultural psychologists have long warned of the danger and limitations concerning IQ tests and the use of scores.

75 Banesh Hoffman, *The Tyranny of Testing* (1967).

76 Robert J. Sternberg, "Toward a Triarchic Theory of Human Intelligence," Behavioral and Brain Sciences 7, no. 2 (1984): 271–273.

77 Brody, 2000; Davidson & Downing, 2000; Sternberg, 1984; Gardner, 1983.

78 A simple search of books yields different intelligences, such as multiple, emotional, cultural, social, successful, creative, spiritual, etc.

79 Gardner originally listed seven candidates for intelligences. Later, he would advocate for an eighth intelligence.

80 Sternberg pointed out that even psychometric theorists themselves held this view (he references Binet and Simon, 1973, and Wechsler, 1958).

81 "It is as much a mistake to exclude testlike behavior from one's view of intelligence as it is to rely upon it exclusively."

82 Thus, Sternberg writes, "The higher order skills of capitalization and compensation may be the same, but what is capitalized on and what is compensated for will vary. The differences across people and situations extend beyond different life paths within a given culture."

83 Sternberg lifts up the example of Ruth D. Feldman's book *Whatever Happened to the Quiz Kids?: Perils and Profits of Growing up Gifted*.

84 Sternberg, "Toward a Triarchic Theory," 273.

85 Goleman calls Gardner's *Frames of Mind* "a manifesto refuting the IQ view," laying a groundwork to explore these personal intelligences. Later Goleman published *Social Intelligence: The Revolutionary New Science of Human Relationships*.

86 Matsumoto and Juang define human culture as "a unique meaning and information system, shared by a group and transmitted across generations, that allows the group to meet basic needs of survival, pursue happiness and well-being, and derive meaning from life."

87 They delineate three stages in the process of cultivating CQ: 1) knowledge: acquiring an understanding of the culture; 2) mindfulness: the ability to pay attention reflectively and creatively to cues to monitor one's own knowledge and feelings; and 3) skills: based on knowledge and mindfulness, the culturally intelligent person develops cross-cultural skills.

88 Contextual intelligence involves understanding all these interactions but also must consider many other factors, some of which are peculiar to a specific context. Further, to help scale our discussion of context, we will employ Wagner's concepts of local and global but extend them in that a global context may be a vast network made of many local contexts, each made up of multiple cultures.

89 According to W. Brian Arthur, who founded complexity economics and works out of the Sante Fe Institute, which studies complex adaptive systems, complex systems have three important characteristics: 1) complex systems grow in co-evolutionary diversity, where different entities compete and collaborate in ever diversified activities, some surviving, while others perish; 2) complex systems are on a continual path of structural deepening, where entities will increase in complexity; and 3) complex systems act as "capturing software," where entities interact with other entities, giving birth to new entities, objects, and events. These three processes help us

understand the complexity of even a seemingly simple context. There is continuous change, a varying degree of predictability, novelty resulting from independent but interrelated actions, and continuous need for adaptation.

90 Michael Polanyi, *Personal Knowledge: Toward a Post-critical Philosophy* (Chicago: University of Chicago Press, 1962), 71.

91 Wagner and Sternberg, 1985.

92 Grotzer and Perkins (2000), cited in Charles H. Brown, Dan Gould, and Sandra Foster, "A Framework for Developing Contextual Intelligence (CI)," Sport Psychologist 19, no. 1 (2005): 51.

93 Margaret J. Wheatley, *Who Do We Choose to Be?: Facing Reality, Claiming Leadership, Restoring Sanity* (Oakland: Berrett-Koehler Publishers, 2017), 160.

94 Alan Hirsch and Mark Nelson, *Reframation: Seeing God, People, and Mission Through Reenchanted Frames* (100 Movements Publishing, 2019), 5.

95 Ibid., 71.

96 Das, 19.

97 Hirsch and Nelson, 72–73.

98 Ibid., 72–73.

99 Crucifixion (San Francisco: HarperOne, 2016), 257

100 David A. DeSilva, *Honor, Patronage, Kinship, and Purity: Unlocking New Testament Culture* (Downers Grove, IL: InterVarsity Press, 2000), 55.

101 Mark J. Edwards, *Ancient Christian Commentary on Scripture: Galatians, Ephesians, Philippians* (Chicago: Fitzroy Dearborn Publishers, 1999), 164.

102 Michael Polanyi, *Personal Knowledge: Towards a Post-Critical Philosophy* (Chicago: University of Chicago Press, 1962), 106.

103 Makoto Matsuo, "Goal Orientation, Critical Reflection, and Unlearning: An Individual-Level Study," Human Resource Development Quarterly 29, no. 1 (2018): 50.

104 Wright, 259.

105 Michael Moynagh, *Church in Life: Innovation, Mission, and Ecclesiology* (Eugene, OR: Cascade, 2018), 143.

106 Ibid., 34.

107 Senge, *The Fifth Discipline*, 13–14.

108 Oliver Sacks, *Awakenings* (Duckworth, 1973), 194–95.

109 For example, Appalachian Christian, Russian Jew, Iranian Muslim.

110 Michael Slaughter, *UnLearning Church* (Nashville: Abingdon, 2008).

111 Gilbert R. Rendle, *Quietly Courageous: Leading the Church in a Changing World* (Lanham, MD: Rowman & Littlefield, 2019), 21–23.

112 Robin Hogarth, Tomás Lejarraga, and Emre Soyer, "The Two Settings of Kind and Wicked Learning Environments," Current Directions in Psychological Science 24, no. 5 (2015): 379, doi: 10.1177/0963721415591878.

113 David J. Epstein, *Range: Why Generalists Triumph in a Specialized World* (New York: Riverhead, 2019), 20–21.

114 A. W. Moore, *The Evolution of Modern Metaphysics: Making Sense of Things* (Cambridge: Cambridge University Press, 2013).

115 Hogarth, Lejarraga, and Soyer, 379.

116 Epstein, 20–21.

117 Robert W. Service, "Leadership and Innovation Across Cultures: The CIQ—Contextual Intelligence Quotient," *Southern Business Review* 37, no. 1 (2012): 25.

118 *Alcoholics Anonymous: The Story of How Many Thousands of Men and Women Have Recovered from Alcoholism* (New York: Alcoholics Anonymous World Services, 2001), xxv.

119 Ibid., xxv–xxxi.

120 Alcoholics Anonymous, "AA Around the World," https://www.aa.org/pages/en_US/aaaround-the-world (accessed June 16, 2020).

121 Matthew J. Crossley, W. Todd Maddox, and F. Gregory Ashby, "Increased Cognitive Load Enables Unlearning in Procedural Category Learning," *Journal of Experimental Psychology: Learning, Memory, and Cognition* 44, no. 11 (2018): 1854.

122 Ibid., 1845.

123 First appeared in the Times Literary Supplement on September 15, 1972, and was penned early in 1945.

124 See https://www.youtube.com/watch?v=mgo7jZzW7Jw.

125 Quoted in Michael Mayne, *The Enduring Melody* (London: Darton, Longman, and Todd, 2006), 144.

126 Paul Taylor, *The Next America: Boomers, Millennials, and the Looming Generational Showdown* (New York: Public Affairs, 2015), p. 39.

127 Graham Cray, *Mission-Shaped Church: Church Planting and Fresh Expressions in a Changing Context* (New York: Seabury Books, 2010).

128 Paul Rezendes, *Tracking and the Art of Seeing: How to Read Animal Tracks and Sign*, 2nd ed. (New York: HarperCollins, 1999), 24.

129 This paragraph and portions of the two that follow are revisions of Leonard Sweet's foreword to Tomas E. Ingram's *Book of Signs: A Crowdsourced Field Guide for Followers of Jesus* (2016).

130 Carol Kaesuk Yoon, *Naming Nature: The Clash between Instinct and Science* (New York: W.W. Norton, 2009), 280.

131 For more on this, see Leonard I. Sweet, *Strong in the Broken Places*.

132 See Peter J. Leithart's book *Traces of the Trinity: Signs of God in Creation and Human Experience* (Ada, MI: Brazos Press, 2015).

133 Jeremy Hance, "The Fragile Songs of the Sumatran Rhinos," AramcoWorld, July/August 2018, 26.

134 Kevin Sharpe and Jon Walgate, "Causality and Creation: The Quantum Footprint," Science and Spirit (November/December 1999), 10.

135 Walter Benjamin long ago said that in this digital age, the distinction between high and popular culture is "altogether obsolete . . . all culture today is popular culture." Although there is more than a grain of truth here, pop art did not totally undo the distinctions between high and folk art.

136 Alan Hirsch, *5Q: Reactivating the Original Intelligence and Capacity of the Body of Christ* (USA: 100M, 2017), xvii.

137 Brown, Gould, and Foster, 59.

138 Brian Eno, quoted in Hirsch, *5Q*, 40.

139 See https://www.definitions.net/definition/scenius.

140 See also *Faithquakes* (1994).

141 See his seascape Helvoetsluys, where Turner added a last-minute touch of red to trump John Constable's elaborate painting of the opening of Waterloo Bridge at the Royal Academy's summer exhibition in 1832.

142 Lorenzo Renzi, *Proust and Vermeer: An Apologia of Imprecision* (2003). For an interview with Renzi, see http://www.essentialvermeer.com/ interviews_newsletter/renzi_interview.html#.XBlVtFxKjZs.

143 Eliade, *The Quest*, 37.

144 William Blake, *Songs of Innocence and of Experience* (1789).

145 Paul Ginsborg, *The Politics of Everyday Life: Making Choices, Changing Lives* (New Haven: Yale University Press, 2005), 110.

146 Frederic Raphael, *Antiquity Matters* (New Haven, CT: Yale University Press, 2017), 151.

147 Lesslie Newbigin, *The Gospel in a Pluralist Society* (Grand Rapids, MI: Eerdmans, 1989), 22.

148 David C. Thomas and Kerr Inkson, *Cultural Intelligence: Surviving and Thriving in the Global Village* (Oakland: Berrett-Koehler, 2017), 41–42.

149 Victor Turner, *The Ritual Process* (1969), 128; "Process, System and Symbol" in *On the Edge of the Bush*, 161.

150 Seth Lerer, *Tradition* (Oxford University Press, 2017).

151 Quoted in Jaroslav Pelikan, *The Vindication of Tradition* (New Haven, CT: Yale University, 1984), 40–41.

152 As quoted in Alan Hirsch, *The Forgotten Ways: Reactivating the Missional Church* (Grand Rapids, MI: Brazos Press, 2006).

153 G. M. Trevelyan, *An Autobiography and Other Essays* (1949).

154 Kutz, *Contextual Intelligence*, 68.

155 Jeanne Liedtka, "Why Design Thinking Works" Harvard Business Review, https://hbr.org/2018/09/why-design-thinking-works (accessed June 16, 2020).

156 Ibid.

157 Michael Beck, D*eep Roots, Wild Branches: Revitalizing the Church in the Blended Ecology* (Franklin, TN: Seedbed Publishing, 2019).

158 For an early book and look at what this might be like for the church to think ahead, see Leonard Sweet, *Carpe Mañana*.

159 *Zondervan Illustrated Commentary*, 392–93.

160 Manuel Castells, *The Rise of the Network Society*, 2nd ed. (London: Wiley Blackwell, 2009), 406.

161 George Lakoff, "Words that Don't Work," Huffington Post, December 7, 2011, https://www.huffpost.com/entry/occupy-rhetoric_b_1133114.

162 Roland Barthes, *Camera Lucida: Reflections on Photography* (New York: Hill and Wang, 2010).

163 Barthes, 42–45.

164 Punctum retains an "aberrant" quality. Barthes himself says, "What I can name cannot really prick me." The inability to name is a good symptom of disturbance and punctum.

165 *Journal of John Wesley,* June 23, 1759.

166 Michael A. Beck, with Jorge Acevedo, *A Field Guide to Methodist Fresh Expressions* (Nashville: Abingdon Press, 2020), 131–32.

167 For more, see Leonard Sweet, 11: *Indispensable Relationships You Can't Be Without* (Colorado Springs, CO: David C. Cook, 2011).

168 Michael L. Davis, "Spiritual Formation: Retrieving Perichoresis as a Model for Shared Leadership in the Marketplace," *Journal of Religious Leadership* 14, no. 1 (2015): 117.

169 Samuel Wells, *Power and Passion: Six Characters in Search of Resurrection* (Grand Rapids, MI: Zondervan, 2007), 20–21.

170 Jackson Wu, *Reading Romans with Eastern Eyes: Honor and Shame in Paul's Message and Mission* (Downers Grove, IL: IVP Academic, 2019), 1.

171 William Temple is the first to cite the word. See Louis Marin, "L'effet sharawadji," in *Traverses*, no. 4–5, Paris (1979).

172 The Bible of dictionaries, the OED, throws up its hands and simply refers the reader to the first place they can find the word in English, which is in William Temple.

173 Jean-François Augoyard and Henry Torgue, *Sonic Experience: A Guide to Everyday Sounds* (Montreal: McGill-Queen's University Press, 2005).

ADDITIONAL RESOURCES

Deep Roots, Wild Branches: Revitalizing the Church in the Blended Ecology
by Michael Beck

Almost everywhere you turn, the story of the Church seems to be one of decline. The painful truth: internal tinkering and tweaks to the status quo will not get us to the kind of church we long for and the kind of community the world craves. Dr. Michael Beck contends we must cultivate what he calls a "blended ecology" of church that has both deep roots and wild branches. Drawing on biblical wisdom and emerging forms of church planting, Beck introduces us to present-day models and examples that don't leave traditional forms behind, but harness the power of "both/and."

From the Steeple to the Street
by Travis Collins

In *From the Steeple to the Street,* Travis Collins addresses the cultural realities behind the Fresh Expressions movement, as well as the movement's theological underpinnings. From practical experience, Collins offers insights to local church leaders on how this might unfold in and through your church.

Fresh Expressions of Church
by Travis Collins

In the last decade, a giant cultural wave has swept the North American church into a brand-new world — a pluralistic, complicated, high-tech/low-touch world. Faced with the challenge of engaging a jaded culture, a fresh expression of church has emerged alongside the traditional church. This short book gives an overview of the Fresh Expressions movement and its innovative approach to reaching those who would perhaps never come to our church buildings.

Dinner Church: Building Bridges by Breaking Bread
by Verlon Fosner

After spending 18 years as a pastor in highly secularized Seattle, Verlon Fosner realized that the traditional ways of doing church were not capable of drawing a secular culture to Jesus. In this struggle, Fosner and his leadership team began to consider the way church was done during the first three centuries, and the sociological implications of doing church around dinner tables.

In *Dinner Church: Building Bridges by Breaking Bread*, Verlon Fosner unveils how the ancient dinner church was rebirthed in his Seattle community and how that vision changed his congregation forever.

Welcome to Dinner, Church
by Verlon Fosner

In its early days, the Church gathered around tables, included the strangers and the poor, ate together and talked about Jesus. While the church of today is very meaningful to Christ-followers, it is failing to help our lost neighbors. This little book examines what it might be like for a traditional church to plant a dinner church in a nearby hurting neighborhood.

Seven Practices for the Church on Mission
by David Fitch

Jesus gave his followers seven key practices: The Lord's Supper, Reconciliation, Proclaiming the gospel, Being with the "least of these," Being with children, Fivefold ministry gifting and Kingdom prayer.

When we practice these disciplines, God becomes faithfully present to us, and we in turn become God's faithful presence to the world. Pastor and professor David Fitch shows how these seven practices can revolutionize the church's presence in our neighborhoods, transform our way of life in the world and advance the kingdom.

IF YOU'RE A FAN OF THIS BOOK, WILL YOU HELP US SPREAD THE WORD?

There are several ways you can help me get the word out about the message of this book...

- Post a 5-Star review on Amazon.

- Write about the book on your Facebook, Twitter, Instagram, LinkedIn, – any social media you regularly use!

- If you blog, consider referencing the book, or publishing an excerpt from the book with a link back to our website. You have our permission to do this as long as you provide proper credit and backlinks.

- Recommend the book to friends – word-of-mouth is still the most effective form of advertising.

- Purchase additional copies to give away as gifts.

The best way to connect is through: www.freshexpressionsus.org

ENJOY THESE OTHER BOOKS BY LEONARD SWEET

- *Rings of Fire: Walking in Faith Through a Volcanic Future*

- *The Bad Habits of Jesus: Showing Us the Way to Live Right in a World Gone Wrong*

- *Tablet to Table: Where Community is Found and Identity Formed*

- *Mother Tongue: How Our Heritage Shapes Our Story*

- *The Jesus Trilogy (with Frank Viola): Jesus Manifesto, Jesus Theography, Jesus Speaks*

ENJOY THESE OTHER BOOKS BY MICHAEL BECK

- *Deep Roots, Wild Branches: Revitalizing the Church in the Blended Ecology*

- *A Field Guide to Methodist Fresh Expressions*

- *Deep and Wild: Re-Missioning Your Church From the Outside In*

You can order these books at www.freshexpressionsus.org or where ever you purchase your favorite books.

Thank you for reading

CONTEXTUAL INTELLIGENCE

UNLOCKING THE ANCIENT SECRET
TO MISSION ON THE FRONT LINES

ABOUT FRESH EXPRESSIONS

Fresh Expressions is an international movement of missionary disciples cultivating new kinds of church alongside existing congregations to more effectively engage our growing post-Christian society.

We equip Christians to revitalize the church by starting contextual expressions of Christian community among the many segments, neighborhoods, and people groups of society.